The Life Cycle of Everyday Stuff

by
Mike Reeske
Shirley Watt Ireton

Featuring *sci*LINKS®—a new way of connecting text and the Internet. Up-to-the-minute online content, classroom ideas, and other materials are just a click away. Go to page xiii to learn more about this new educational resource.

NSTA press
NATIONAL SCIENCE TEACHERS ASSOCIATION
ARLINGTON, VIRGINIA

Published with support from the United States Environmental Protection Agency

NATIONAL SCIENCE TEACHERS ASSOCIATION

Shirley Watt Ireton, Director
Beth Daniels, Managing Editor
Judy Cusick, Associate Editor
Jessica Green, Assistant Editor
Anne Early, Editorial Assistant

Art and Design
Linda Olliver, Director
NSTA Web
Tim Weber, Webmaster
Periodicals Publishing
Shelley Carey, Director
Printing and Production
Catherine Lorrain-Hale, Director
Publications Operations
Erin Miller, Manager
*sci*LINKS
Tyson Brown, Manager

National Science Teachers Association
Gerald F. Wheeler, Executive Director
David Beacom, Publisher

NSTA Press, NSTA Journals, and the NSTA Web site deliver high-quality resources for science educators.

The Life Cycle of Everyday Stuff
NSTA Stock Number: PB154X
ISBN 0-87355-187-7
Library of Congress Card Number: 00-110013
Printed in the USA by Automated Graphic Systems
Printed on recycled paper.

Table of Contents

Introduction

Unit One: What Is a Life Cycle?

Unit Two: Dissecting a Telephone—Design

Unit Three: Raw Materials—
Acquisition and Processing

Unit Four: Manufacturing a Product

Unit Five: The Useful Life of a Product

Unit Six: A Tale of Two Cups—Disposal and Reuse

Unit Seven: Redesigning a Product

Appendix A

The Life Cycle of Everyday Stuff

Sustainable Development

In 1990, the World Commission on Environment and Development, a group developed by the United Nations, defined sustainable development as "development that meets the needs of the present without compromising the ability of future generations to meet their needs." Sustainable development is a process that balances both industrial and economic growth. It takes a broad systems view of what sustains economies, the environment, and human life. It looks at ways to sustain the quality of life for all people of the Earth at a level that will allow a balance between economic health, environmental health, and societal health. Life cycle assessment uses the goals of sustainable development and applies them in a practical way to the design, manufacturing, use, and end-of-life options of any product to make it more "environmentally friendly" and, in the end, more sustainable both now and in the future.

Topic: sustainable development

Go to: www.scilinks.org

Code: LCS01

Why Investigate the Life Cycle of Products?

The National Science Teachers Association (NSTA), using a grant from the Environmental Protection Agency (EPA), designed these instructional units to help you and your students explore a new tool—*life cycle assessment*. Parallel to living things, material products also have a "birth, life, and death"—a life cycle. For a material product, these steps include design, raw materials, manufacturing and distributing, useful life, and disposal or reuse. Life cycle assessment is a relatively new tool for science and economics. A life cycle assessment (LCA)—also called a *cradle-to-grave analysis*—looks at the environmental impact of the total life of a product. Its goals are to minimize the product's negative or unplanned effects and maximize the product's usefulness and profit. With these goals, the design of the product ultimately affects each stage of its life cycle. This book uses common products, such as the telephone, to illustrate how LCA works.

Examination of the life cycle of a product also offers a systematic way to look at the flow of energy and matter through the Earth's system—a physical science parallel to food webs. In the context of life cycles, these units use central science concepts to explore the energy, raw materials, and waste issues that are part of the history of any manufactured product. As students consider the trade-offs made at each life cycle step, they will learn to recognize the decisions made by the producer to balance economic, environmental, and developmental needs. In addition, they'll have opportunities to make parallel decisions about products they design and use.

These trade-off decisions are necessary in the goal of *sustainable development*. What is sustainable development? According to the President's Council on Sustainable Development (1997): "A sustainable United States will have a growing economy that provides equitable opportunities for satisfying livelihoods and a safe, healthy, high quality of life for current and future generations. Our nation will protect its environment, its natural resource base, and the functions and viability of natural systems on which all life depends." This goal of sustainable development calls upon educators to expand American students' conceptual awareness and take a systems view of what we use, how we use it, and how it is disposed.

As this country becomes more technologically advanced, it is essential for students to clearly see the important connections between a relatively small group of the Earth's raw materials and the products we value. For example, petroleum powers the industries of our planet. However, few students understand that plastics are synthesized from refined petroleum. Nor do they understand that the energy to produce nitrogen fertilizers is mostly generated from fossil fuels—a non-renewable resource.

Life cycle assessment gives students the opportunity to see these important connections in natural and human-made systems. It allows them to make informed decisions about the allocation of limited natural resources in the future, as these resources diminish in size and their dollar costs escalate. These types of decisions, based on the best science available, are the foundations of science literacy in our high school curriculum. It is our hope that the use of these materials in your classroom will contribute to the goals of science literacy for the 21st century.

What Is Life Cycle Assessment?

Life cycle assessment originated in the early 1960s as workers tried to develop materials and energy inventories to estimate the environmental impacts of product manufacture. During the 1980s, Europe's Green Movement reawakened interest in LCAs. The Green Party called for a complete restructuring of social, cultural, and political life, especially in the developed countries. Today, it looks at important issues from the standpoint of the environment. The result—European manufacturers now routinely take back and reuse or recycle products such as cars. According to the Green Movement, examining life cycles is an important part of understanding the relatedness of all issues.

Around the same time in the United States, several consulting firms conducted landmark studies on solid waste. They analyzed the lives of common products such as foam and paper cups, disposable and cloth diapers, and plastic and paper grocery bags, using a cradle-to-grave analysis of energy and waste impacts at each stage of the product's life.

These studies included some surprising answers to hotly debated environmental issues related to organic versus synthetic products. They found that plastic cups, because they were uniformly made of a single material—polystyrene—are less energy consuming and easier to recycle than the paper cup. They also produce less total waste.

Life cycle assessment is now an important tool for technology and planning, as our solid waste disposal options dwindle and energy prices continue to increase. LCA is only one type of this increasingly popular method of sustainable design. Other processes include eco-balance, resource analysis, and Environmental Impact Assessment (EIA). However, LCA goes one step further and evaluates the inventory. This step provides a quantitative catalog of the inputs (energy and raw materials) and outputs (including environmental releases) for a specific product, process, or activity. These are then used to evaluate such things as environmental effects, site selection for manufacturing and distribution, habitat alteration, good management practices, worker health concerns, community relations, and public perception. Once an evaluation is complete, the company or agency rates the results and develops an action plan to sustain economic growth while also sustaining the environment.

Why a Systems View?

Within a given system, the components are related to each other in defined ways. Until recently, students examined each separate component, but rarely were given the opportunity to look at the overarching relationships between them. Science teaching was based on memorizing facts. In the early 1990s, an emerging consensus among science educators brought about the implementation of more thematic and integrated science programs. These programs emphasized the relationships between the major scientific disciplines by using such broad concepts as energy, evolution, and systems and interactions. In a parallel fashion, the concept of sustainable human development emerged.

How to Use This Book

The chapters in this book are organized around the stages in the life cycle of a product:

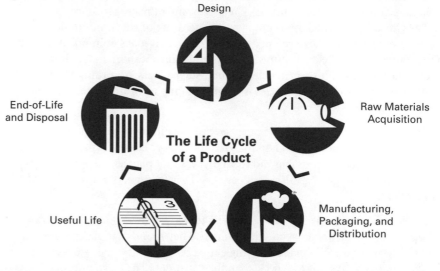

Instructional Design and Science Standards

The authors assembled the units of *The Life Cycle of Everyday Things* using a "backwards" instructional design based on a process developed by Jay McTighe and Grant Wiggins and published by the Association for Supervision and Curriculum Development as *Understanding by Design*. Using this method, the authors evaluated the levels of knowledge that the units could address. In nearly any topic, in any area of study, there is typically far more content than can or should reasonably be presented to students. This design method provides a method to discriminate among three levels of content: *Enduring Understandings, Important to Know and Do, and Worth Being Familiar With.* These three levels established the curricular priorities—the Learning Goals—on which to build the units.

The Enduring Understandings identified for each unit are core to the *National Science Education Standards* and the *Benchmarks for Science Literacy*, and are required for understanding of each stage of a product's life cycle. These enduring understandings are the ones that have value beyond the classroom, and that are transferable to new situations.

As a second level of content, the authors identified the important knowledge (facts, concepts, and principles) and skills (processes, strategies, and methods) that students should master in order to understand the content of the unit. The Objectives for each unit are derived from these first and second levels of content.

As a third level of content, the authors identified content that was just worth being familiar with, perhaps that added perspective or detail. Content worth being familiar with was built into the units in a broad-brush way: included as sidebars or extensions.

Once the authors identified the relevant content for each life cycle unit, the instructional methods for each unit were established. The authors built the instructional delivery methods to account for a variety of learning styles. The constructivist principles of identifying what students understand, and providing students with opportunities to challenge and modify these preconceptions as they learn, were used in each unit, and in the overall design of the book.

The Learning Goals for each unit are at the end of the teacher sections, accompanied by the relevant National Science Education Standards and Benchmarks for Science Literacy. Most state or district science standards are correlated to these standards, and you'll find online correlations on several Web sites. These standards may guide your selection of when to use *The Life Cycle of Everyday Stuff* with your classes, and provide pointers toward using the concepts of life cycle assessments with other science instruction.

Unit Overviews

The activities in this book are suitable for secondary Earth science, environmental science, physical science, or integrated science classes. Unit Three may also be suitable for chemistry classes.

Unit One: What Is a Life Cycle? introduces the concepts of a life cycle using the *Life Cycle of a Pencil* poster. Through class discussion, the class extends the ideas of this visual depiction to other common items and learns that all products have origins and fates—a life cycle. They then focus on the matter and energy transformations at each life cycle step—a process that develops student ability to see a product as part of a cycle. Students will explore what they already know about product life cycles, and complete a pretest of their current understanding that they will revisit and modify in the final unit.

In **Unit Two: Dissecting a Telephone—Design**, students discover that a simple product (e.g., a polystyrene cup) and a complicated product (e.g., a computer) each must have a design that relates structure and function. This design is the result of the synthesis of several perspectives: historical developments in the use of the product or products with a similar function, energy expenditure, environmental impact, and product economics. Students consider the structure and function of major telephone components. They are then introduced to the roles they will use throughout the remaining units to develop a way of understanding how the design process influences every stage in the life cycle of a product.

Students next answer two questions about telephones and, indirectly, about all products: What are they made of, and why? **Unit Three: Raw Materials—Acquisition and Processing** examines the second stage in the life cycle—raw materials, and uses a literature search to explore various aspects of three of the main materials in a telephone: plastic, metals, and silicon chips. Through a laboratory experiment, students model the extraction of metal from ore.

Unit Four: Manufacturing a Product discusses the step in the life cycle that creates final products out of raw materials. Students make a protective package for a frozen dessert and then consider materials and design options. They then weigh the energy, economic, and environmental impacts of their package to highlight the trade-offs and decision-making needed at each stage of the life cycle of a product.

Unit Five: The Useful Life of a Product explores the fourth stage in a product's life cycle. Students examine issues of durability, depreciation, and waste as they evaluate this part of a product's life cycle. The class will use mathematical and economic concepts to illustrate the useful life of some common household products. As an optional extension activity, students can conduct original research by following the useful life of a school telephone.

What happens to a product when it no longer works and its useful life is over? The last stage in a product's life cycle is disposal or reuse—called the *end-of-life* stage. **Unit Six: A Tale of Two Cups—Disposal and Reuse** has students examine the trade-offs involved in selecting one drinking cup over another. They investigate what would happen to each type of cup as a waste and review the concept of life cycles as a way to consider waste management issues. Students then analyze the end-of-life stage for a telephone. What happens to each component of a phone?

How can materials be redesigned to incorporate economic and environmental criteria into their life cycle? In Unit Seven: Redesigning a Product, students examine the strengths and weaknesses of the life cycle assessment tool to incorporate different values in the design of a product. They use a telephone to examine the practice of sustainable design and then develop their own criteria for evaluating a product. This unit is an embedded assessment of student learning. Student teams present the results of their research that began in Unit One. By analyzing how the design of the telephone relates to each stage of its life cycle, students are able to synthesize the basic concepts of this book.

Group Work

In *The Life Cycle of Everyday Stuff,* much of the student work will be done in teams. Science is a cooperative endeavor, and teamwork allows students to engage in that mix of individual thought and cooperative exchange that is real scientific investigation.

Also, the team approach offers an opportunity for students to explore viewpoints and debate ideas. There are several non-contradictory ways to view each stage of a product life cycle, and each viewpoint has a particular value at each stage. Units Two, Three, Four, and Five have "Expert Roles" handouts for students. These handouts provide questions to guide a member of each team to examine how History, Design, Energy Flow, Environmental Impact, and Economics play a role at each stage of a manufactured product's "life." Student journals provide a record for answers, and team/class discussions and team presentations provide the forum for exchange of practical ideas.

The teacher's role during much of the group work will be as facilitator. You may wish to circulate among the teams as they are working together, providing suggestions for resources and perhaps changing the direction of a discussion.

Using a Journal

A lab journal will help students organize, analyze, and interpret the information they collect throughout the course of their investigations. The journal will not only provide students with a record of how their knowledge grows, but will provide you with a mechanism for assessing student performance, understanding, and application of knowledge. Journals enable students to organize information as they gather it, to share it with peers, and to integrate class information toward successful participation in the culminating activities. Writing also helps students develop ideas, think through problems, make decisions, and determine what remains to be discovered.

Students can use a separate notebook or a section of a three-ring binder for their journals. This allows for organization and for containment of single sheets that can be easily turned in for grading. Organization is a critical learning skill for all students, and journals must be organized to be useful and meaningful. You may want students to number each page and construct a table of contents for their journals.

Assessment

The units have a mix of instructional techniques—class discussion, group discussion, group and individual assignments, group and individual presentations, homework questions, lab work, and independent research projects. Build rubrics to measure what your students are learning based on your own instructional goals and on the "Enduring Understandings" and "Important Facts and Skills" guides at the end of each Teacher Section. Unit Seven, Redesigning a Product, concludes with group presentations of their design work, and includes a multi-trait rubric to share with students to guide their presentation development. You may wish to use Unit Seven as a summative assessment of student learning in the previous units.

Assessments are the techniques to analyze student accomplishment against the Enduring Understandings and Important Facts and Skills curricular priorities of the unit. Many of the student tasks in *The Life Cycle of Everyday Stuff* serve as authentic assessments—they are designed to have students simulate or replicate important real-world challenges. In Unit Four: Manufacturing a Product, for example, students design, build, test, and redesign a simple product, gaining first-hand knowledge of the challenges and illustrating their mastery of the process.

Journals are also important tools for assessment. Students should record all observations and activity results and include the separate student worksheets in their journals. In addition to answering specific questions, encourage students to record any thoughts related to the issues covered in this book. You can use the journals to assess students' abilities to conduct the activities, their knowledge of the significance of the activities, their understanding of the results and what they have learned, and their abilities to use this information. Students will record their pretest of their life cycle knowledge in their journals in Unit One. You may wish to encourage students to revisit this pretest to have them concretely mark their gains of understanding throughout the course of these units.

Life Cycle of a Pencil Poster Insert

Several units of *The Life Cycle of Everyday Stuff* suggest using the *Life Cycle of a Pencil* poster, included with this book, as a visual reference of the parts of a life cycle. This poster was initially designed for, and included with, *Science Scope*, NSTA's journal for middle level science teachers. Use it to broaden students' awareness of product life cycles. A small black and white version of the poster is included as an appendix.

*sci*LINKS

The Life Cycle of Everyday Stuff brings you *sci*LINKS, a creative project from NSTA that blends the best of the two main educational "drivers"—textbooks and telecommunications—into a dynamic new educational tool for all children, their parents, and their teachers. This *sci*LINKS effort links specific textbook and supplemental resource locations with instructionally rich Internet resources. As you and your students use sciLINKS, you will find rich new pathways for learners, new opportunities for professional growth among teachers, and new modes of engagement for parents.

In this *sci*LINKed text, you will find an icon near several of the concepts you are studying. Under it, you will find the *sci*LINKS URL (http://www.sciLINKS.org/) and a code. Go to the *sci*LINKS Web site, sign in, type the code from your text, and you will receive a list of URLs that are selected by science educators. Sites are chosen for accurate and age-appropriate content and good pedagogy. The underlying database changes constantly eliminate dead or revised sites or simply replace them with better selections. The ink may dry on the page, but the science it describes will always be fresh.

Acknowledgments

NSTA, and authors Mike Reeske and Shirley Watt Ireton, would like to thank the many people who contributed to the development of *The Life Cycle of Everyday Stuff*. First to EPA's Office of Solid Waste, whose funding and vision made the project possible. OSW staff Pat Washington, Judi Kane, and Barbara Roth all worked to make this project possible. Thank you next to the advisory panel of Keith Wheeler, Judy Baldridge, Nancy Ridenour, Kathleen Kaye, and EPA's Patty Whiting, who brought their broad knowledge of science, science education, and the environment to bear in developing the plan for this book. Christina Frasch Findlay brought talent and enthusiasm to the coordination of the development process.

Thanks, then, to manuscript reviewers Cathy Boucvalt of John Curtis Christian School in River Ridge, Louisiana; Darrel Boenig of Ben Franklin High School in New Orleans, Louisiana; Susie Shields, Environmental Education coordinator for the Oklahoma Department of Environmental Quality in Oklahoma City, Oklahoma; Scott and Zelda Martin of Putnam City High School in Oklahoma City, Oklahoma; Judy Reeves of Baldwin County High School in Bay Minette, Alabama; and Debbie Dahl of Moore High School in Moore, Oklahoma. Patricia Washington of EPA provided research, resources, and guidance, and coordinated the manuscript review within EPA.

Tom Diener of Marshall School, Duluth, Minnesota; Sue Ellen Lyons of Holy Cross School, New Orleans, Louisiana; Jane Brandt of Kellog Middle School, Rochester, Minnesota; Tomas Rodriguez of Webb Middle School, Austin, Texas; Marie Pool of Clinton High School, Clinton, Oklahoma, and their students provided invaluable feedback as field testers of the manuscript.

Mike and Shirley both thank their families for their support during the writing of this book.

Graves Fowler Associates provided the art and layout; cover illustration is by Elizabeth Brandt; inside illustrations by Joan Waites. *The Life Cycle of Everyday Stuff* is produced by NSTA Press: Shirley Watt Ireton, director; Beth Daniels, managing editor; Judy Cusick, associate editor; Jessica Green, assistant editor. Anne Early and Jessica Green were project editors for *The Life Cycle of Everyday Stuff*.

The site selection process involves four review stages:

1. First, a cadre of undergraduate science education majors searches the World Wide Web for interesting science resources. The undergraduates submit about 500 sites a week for consideration.

2. Next, packets of these Web pages are organized and sent to teacher-Web watchers with expertise in given fields and grade levels. The teacher-Web watchers can also submit Web pages they have found on their own. The teachers pick the jewels from this selection and correlate them to the National Science Education Standards. These pages are submitted to the *sci*LINKS database.

3. Then scientists review these correlated sites for accuracy.

4. Finally, NSTA staff approves the Web pages and edits the information provided for accuracy and consistent style.

Who pays for *sci*LINKS? *sci*LINKS is a free service for textbook and supplemental resource users, but obviously, someone must pay for it. Participating publishers pay a fee to NSTA for each book that contains *sci*LINKS. The program is also supported by a grant from the National Aeronautics and Space Administration.

About the Authors

Mike Reeske has taught science in high schools for over 30 years and currently teaches Chemistry and Integrated Science at Vista High School in Vista, California, where he is the Science Department Chairman. He was the former Director of Education for the Orange County Marine Institute and is currently a teacher-developer for the Science Education for Public Understanding Program (SEPUP) at the Lawrence Hall of Science, University of California at Berkeley. He has co-authored many SEPUP modules and several books including *Issues, Evidence and You* and *Science and Sustainability*, from which his current interest in life cycle assessment has come.

Shirley Watt Ireton is Director of the National Science Teachers Association Press and NSTA's Environment Education Coordinator. For the past 16 years she has developed and managed science education projects with EPA, USGS, NASA, National Park Service, USDA, Medtronic Corporation, Abbott Laboratories, and many others. The results of these projects have been numerous award-winning publications for science educators. Her interests are conveying leading-edge science to educators in classroom-ready ways, and modeling innovative teaching techniques in the development of science education publications.

What Is a Life Cycle?

Summary

Just as living things go through a series of developmental stages from birth to death, products must also complete a life cycle—from design to disposal. However, the cycle does not stop with the end of life. In nature, living things die and serve as energy for animals, plants, and bacteria. Likewise, used products can be recycled into new products, or simply discarded as waste. In both cases, matter and energy are conserved.

Unit One introduces these concepts using the *Life Cycle of a Pencil* poster. Through class discussion, you'll extend the ideas on this visual depiction to other common classroom items to emphasize that all products have origins and fates—a life cycle. As a class, and then as homework, students review and apply their knowledge of the properties of matter and energy to the series of transformations that make up the life cycle of a product.

Objectives

- To introduce the concepts of life cycles

- To emphasize that all products have a life cycle

- To apply knowledge of the properties of matter and energy to the series of transformations that make up the life cycle of a product

Preparation

Before class begins, place the objects on a table where students can clearly see them as they enter the room. You may substitute other objects, but keep the telephone. Display the *Life Cycle of a Pencil* poster. Duplicate enough copies of **Student Sheet 1.1, Introduction to Life Cycles—Matter and Energy Transformations**, and **Student Sheet 1.2, What's in a Product and Where Does It Go?** You may need to do some research in advance for the questions on **Student Sheet 1.2**, but this sheet is a starting point record for students' thinking about product life cycles.

Teaching Sequence

Day One

Step One: Ask the class to analyze the objects on the table according to the following three criteria: Where did the raw materials come from to make this object? How long is the product useful? What happens to it when humans don't find it useful any longer? This should be a quick discussion, recording opinions on the board or on an overhead. (Use the following table as a format, but the short discussion should focus on the life cycle process, not on filling in the cells.)

Step Two: Use the *Life Cycle of a Pencil* poster as a guide. Hold up the pencil and have students examine their own pencil. Ask students what they think the pencil is made of, and fill in student answers in the Raw Materials column. The sidebar, "There's No Lead in Pencils!" provides some background for the discussion. Ask students where the pencil's raw materials come from, how the pencil arrived in the student's possession, and where the pencil will end up. Students should realize that some products have many origins, and that even a simple product like a pencil can be the result of a variety of natural resources and human labor from all over the world. Use the poster to elicit and reinforce student contributions.

Students should realize that the time they spend interacting with an object is only a portion of the "life span" of that object.

Product	Raw materials	Useful life	Then what?
Pencil			
T-shirt			
Soda can			
Newspaper			
Telephone			
Phone book			
Disposable diaper			

Time Management

Two class periods

Materials

- A telephone that has ended its useful life
- Pencils
- T-shirt
- Several objects commonly discarded by most students daily (e.g., milk cartons, soda cans, a polystyrene foam cup, a newspaper)
- *Life Cycle of a Pencil* poster
- A plant, preferably with flowers or seeds

SCI**LINKS**®

THE WORLD'S A CLICK AWAY

Topic: life cycle of a pencil

Go to: www.scilinks.org

Code: LCS02

Step Three: When the level of discussion indicates that students are comfortable with the idea of a pencil having a life cycle, draw attention to life cycles in nature. Ask students for examples of life cycles in nature (humans, animals, plants). Record their answers on the board or an overhead.

Use the plant to illustrate a parallel flow with raw materials (seed, water, root support); manufacturing (sunlight, nutrients, water); useful life (continued growth, seed production); end-of-life (death); and reuse (decomposition and return to nutrients that may be used by other organisms). You may wish to sketch the cycle of the plant to guide the discussion.

In an Earth science context, continue this parallel with the water cycle, nitrogen cycle, or carbon cycle. In a biology or environmental science context, revisit what students already know about composting, or more explicitly, food webs. Students should realize that life cycles are pervasive in the world around them.

Step Four: Distribute **Student Sheet 1.1, Introduction to Life Cycles— Matter and Energy Transformations**.

Introduce the *Law of Conservation of Matter:* In all physical and chemical changes, matter is neither created nor destroyed, but it may be converted from one form to another.

Relate this to the *First Law of Thermodynamics*—the Conservation of Energy: In all physical and chemical changes, energy is neither created nor destroyed, but it may be converted from one form to another.

Finally, further the idea of energy flow by introducing the *Second Law of Thermodynamics*—when energy is changed from one form to another, some of the useful energy is always degraded to lower-quality, more-dispersed, less-useful energy. Students will revisit these concepts throughout *The Life Cycle of Everyday Stuff* as they consider energy flow as part of each stage of the life cycle of an object.

Have students reproduce the *Life Cycle of a Pencil* in their lab journal. As directed in **Student Sheet 1.1**, students write a sentence describing the changes in energy and matter at each stage of the cycle.

Day Two
Step Five: As a class, review the homework. Assess student's general understanding of matter and energy transformations in their diagrams by checking to see if they have shown the following at each stage: 1) energy inputs; 2) material inputs; 3) waste outputs; and 4) waste energy as heat. Look for broad, general categories. Suggest to the class that energy is lost at each stage. Where does this happen? Develop the idea of heat loss and have them add arrows to their diagram to show this.

Step Six: Draw students' attention again to the telephone. Hand out **Student Sheet 1.2, What's in a Product and Where Does It Go?** Students should examine the telephone in groups as they each fill out **Student Sheet 1.2**. Have them keep both sheets in their lab journal.

These short questions are a pretest to the life cycle material and a guide for students to apply the thinking they have just done on the life cycle of a pencil to the life cycle of a telephone. Students should realize there are no right or wrong answers to these questions.

Use student answers to gauge where you need to place your emphasis in teaching the rest of *Life Cycle*. Students should keep this sheet in their lab journal. After completing Unit Seven, students can review their answers to **Student Sheet 1.2** to see what they have learned.

There's No Lead in Pencils!

Contrary to popular belief, pencils do not contain lead. Lead was used in pencils throughout the 19th century, but was abandoned because it was too soft and left only a light mark on the writing surface. Lead is also a toxic heavy metal that can be hazardous to human health. In 1820, Joseph Dixon developed a process of mixing clay with graphite to make the writing cores pencils still use today. The graphite-clay mixture is blended and extruded into pencil-sized "leads." The leads are baked at 982°C to make the material smooth and hard.

The wooden part of a pencil is made by cutting a block of cedar wood into slats. The slats are stained on one side and grooves are cut into one surface. The leads are placed into the grooves, a second cedar slat is placed on top, and the two slats are glued together. This "pencil sandwich" is milled to separate the individual pencils. Each pencil is painted and lettered. A metal band called a *ferrule* is crimped onto the end, and the eraser is crimped into the ferrule to finish the pencil. The eraser was once made of rubber, but vinyl plastic and synthetic rubber mixed with pumice has replaced the rubber.

Learning Goals

Unit One has been constructed to guide student understanding of the following Learning Goals.

Enduring understandings

- *Life cycles are parallel in living and non-living things.*

- *Matter has characteristic properties that are related to composition and structure.*

- *In all physical and chemical changes, matter and energy are neither created nor destroyed, but may be converted from one form to another.*

- *When energy changes from one form to another, some of the useful energy is always degraded to lower-quality, more-dispersed, less-useful energy.*

- *Materials from human societies affect both the physical and chemical cycles of the Earth.*

Important facts and skills

- *Products can be categorized by their raw materials and by what happens to those raw materials.*

- *The five basic areas of life cycle assessment are: design; materials acquisition; manufacture and transportation; use and maintenance; and recycling and waste disposal.*

- *Energy, human impact, and waste production are part of a complex system that influences each step of the cycle.*

These Unit One Learning Goals contribute to student learning of the following *National Science Education Standards* and *Benchmarks for Science Literacy*.

National Science Education Standards

Unifying Concepts and Processes
    Systems, order, and organization
Physical Science: Content Standard B
    Structure and properties of matter
    Conservation of energy
    Interactions of energy and matter
Life Science: Content Standard C
    Matter, energy, and organization in living things
Earth and Space Science: Content Standard D
    Geochemical cycles
Science in Personal and Social Perspectives: Content Standard F
    Natural resources
    Environmental quality: Material from human societies affects both physical and chemical cycles of the Earth

Benchmarks for Science Literacy

4 The Physical Setting
      4D Structure of matter
      4E Energy transformations
5 The Living Environment
      5E Flow of matter and energy
7 Human Society
      7E Social trade-offs
8 The Designed World
      8B Materials and manufacturing
      8C Energy sources and use
11 Common Themes
      11A Systems

Resources

LIFE CYCLES

Publications

Bower, M., and L. Warren. 1999. *The Consumer's Guide to Effective Environmental Choices.* New York: Union of Concerned Scientists.

Fava, J. A., Denison, R., Jones, B., Curran, M. A., Vogon, B., Selke, S., and Barnum, J., eds. 1991. *A Technical Framework for Life-Cycle Assessment.* Pensacola, Florida: Society of Environmental Technology and Chemistry.

Hunt, R.G., and W.E. Franklin. 1996. LCA—how it came about: personal reflections on the development of LCA in the USA. *International Journal of Life Cycle Assessment* 1:4–7.

Hunt, R.G., Sellers, J., and W.E. Franklin. 1992. Resource and environmental profile analysis: A life cycle assessment for products and procedures. *Environmental Impact Assessment Review* 12:245–269.

U.S. Environmental Protection Agency. 1993. *Life-Cycle Assessment: Inventory Guidelines and Principles.* Prepared for EPA by Battelle and Franklin Associates, Ltd. Washington, DC. EPA/600/R-92/245.

Web Sites

Franklin Associates, Ltd., Life Cycle Assessment: http://www.fal.com/LCA/lca.html

The International Institute for Sustainable Development, Life Cycle Assessment Technique: http://iisd.ca/business/lifecycle.htm

Society of Environmental Toxicology and Chemistry, Life Cycle Assessment: http://www.setac.org/lca.html

PENCILS
Web Sites

The General Pencil Company: http://www.generalpencil.com/

The Tennessee Pencil Company: http://www.tennesseepencil.com/

TELEPHONES
Publications

Meyer, R.O. 1995. *Old-Time Telephones! Technology, Restoration and Repair.* New York: TAB Books.

Web Sites

Antique Telephone History: http://www.cybercomm.net/~chuck/phones.html

Invention & Design, Telephone Module: http://jefferson.village.virginia.edu/~meg3c/id/id_telmod.html

Private Line's Telephone History: http://www.privateline.com/TelephoneHistory/History1.htm

Tribute to the Telephone: http://hyperarchive.lcs.mit.edu/telecom-archives/tribute/

Note: Web sites current as of August, 2000.

Videos

Biography: "Alexander Graham Bell: Voice of Invention" AAE-14146 (available through http://store.biography.com/)

Biography: "Modern Marvels: The Telephone" AAE-12230 (available through http://store.biography.com/)

PBS Home Video: "The American Experience: The Telephone" 2447-WEBHV (available through PBS Home Video at http://shop.pbs.org/MDTQvsVN7s/products/A2447/)

Introduction to Life Cycles— Matter and Energy Transformations

Law of Conservation of Matter

In all physical and chemical changes, matter is neither created nor destroyed, but it may be converted from one form to another.

(It's all still here.)

First Law of Thermodynamics

In all physical and chemical changes, energy is neither created nor destroyed, but it may be converted from one form to another.

(You can't get something for nothing.)

Second Law of Thermodynamics

When energy is changed from one form to another, some of the useful energy is always degraded to lower-quality, more-dispersed, less-useful energy.

(You can't break even.)

Directions

On a separate sheet of paper in your Lab Journal, **draw a circle and fill in the stages from the *Life Cycle of a Pencil* poster.** At each stage of its life cycle the product is changing. Its matter may be converted from one form to another, energy may be added to the product, and energy may be released. Based on what you know of the life cycle of a pencil, **write a paragraph describing the changes in matter and energy at each stage of its life cycle.**

What's in a Product and Where Does It Go?

The study you are about to begin will challenge you to examine the social and natural resource issues related to the design and use of a common product—the telephone. This is your initial look at the issues, a reference point for you to use to gauge your own intellectual growth. These questions ask about your current knowledge of the material in this unit. **Record your answers in your lab journal.**

Consider a telephone.

1. List as many materials as you can think of that might be part of a telephone.

2. For the materials you listed in Question 1, are there other materials that could have been substituted for them 10 years ago? Fifty years ago? One hundred years ago?

3. Raw materials are either grown or taken from the Earth. For example, copper is a raw material; wire is not. List as many of the raw materials as you can that might have been used to make the materials you listed in Question 1.

4. What energy may have been used to make these materials?

5. Was energy used to get the telephone from its manufacturing point to where it is now?

6. How long does a telephone last before it is disposed of?

7. What could happen to this telephone if it breaks?

8. Does the telephone have pieces that could be recycled or reused?

9. What pieces would produce the most waste if they were thrown away? How long will it take to decompose?

10. Using the life cycle of a pencil as a model, sketch the components in the life cycle of a telephone.

Dissecting a Telephone—Design

Objectives

- To explore the first stage in the life cycle of a product—design

- To investigate the relationship of structure and function in product design

- To develop a way of understanding how the design process influences every stage in the life cycle of a product.

- To investigate the interrelationship of issues—history, energy flow, environmental impact, and economics—that influence product design

- To introduce the expert roles used in the remaining units

Summary

A product's life cycle originates with design. A simple product (e.g., a polystyrene cup) and a complicated product (e.g., a computer) must have a design that relates structure and function. This design is the result of the synthesis of several perspectives: historical developments in the use of the product or products with a similar function; energy expenditure; environmental impact; and product economics.

This unit guides students to consider the structure and function of major telephone components. Students are then introduced to the roles or perspectives that will be used throughout the remaining units to develop a way of understanding how the design process influences every stage in the life cycle of a product like the telephone.

Figure 2.1: A telephone

Time Management
Two class periods

Materials
- Old telephones
- Flathead screwdriver
- Phillips screwdriver
- Needle-nose pliers
- Small magnet

Preparation

Obtain at least one old telephone at a thrift store, from your local telephone company, or ask students to bring in an old broken telephone they have at home. The phones do not need to be the same type. If you are able to find several old phones, you'll be able to give one to each team of five students. Perform at least a partial telephone dissection yourself to determine how long the activity will take, what tools are needed, and the kind of questions students may ask.

You do not need to be an expert on phone components, but should know the basic structure of a telephone and how it works. If appropriate for the class you are teaching, you may wish to spend part of a class period reviewing the physics and technology of telephone function at the start of the unit, then revisit students' new knowledge of telephone function at the end. If this is not your field, another teacher may be willing to help review telephone function with your class.

Students need only a general understanding about how a telephone works to handle this unit. They will answer many of their own questions as the unit progresses.

Put together a student disassembly team—a small group of students who will each remove one or two telephone parts and lead a short class discussion of the function of that component. Ask for volunteers before class, or select five or six students on your own.

If you anticipate your class will have difficulty beginning with the complex set of components in the telephone, you might want to introduce this activity by having them take apart something much simpler, such as a used tape or video cassette. They can open these easily with a screwdriver and lay the components out and then decide what each is made of and what function it performs.

Teaching Sequence

Day One

Step One: Most telephones have the same main components: microphone, speaker, power cord, data entry method, printed circuit board, base or stand, cover. While looking at the complete telephone, have class members identify the functions that must happen to make a telephone work (sending, receiving, energy input, structural support, data entry, controls, protection, etc.). List the components and functions on the board or overhead.

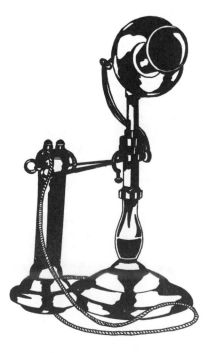

Tell students they will more fully investigate what the components are made of in another step—this is their preliminary look.

Step Two: Distribute **Student Sheet 2.1, The Structure and Materials of a Telephone**. Make an overhead from this handout or draw the grid on the board. Stress that this dissection is no different from a biological dissection. Students should use the same care in removal, recording notes in their lab journal during the dissection.

Step Three: Have the student disassembly team come to the front of the class. Using the tools provided, one student at a time should carefully remove one component, but leave any wire connection in place, so that the phone can be loosely reconstructed. As the student detaches the part, she describes what she is doing and leads the discussion for the class to determine the component's function and raw materials. Students add this information to their grids. After the class has discussed the dissected component, the disassembly team member passes the tools on to the next person.

The following is a sample grid for what your class will develop. Components are included as examples, but are not intended to be an exhaustive list.

Sample Student Sheet 2.1

The Structure and Materials of a Telephone

Component	Function(s)	Structure (raw materials)
Microphone	Sending	Iron, plastic
Handset cord	Sending, receiving	Copper, plastic
Speaker	Sending, receiving	Paper, iron, plastic
Wall cord	Energy input	Copper, plastic
Screws	Structural support	Steel
Handset	Structural support	Plastic
Plastic cover	Structural support, protection	Plastic
Key pad	Data entry	Plastic
Circuit board	Controls	Silicon, copper, other metals
Wiring	Controls	Copper, aluminum

Topic: Alexander G. Bell

Go to: www.scilinks.org

Code: LCS03

Step Four: Split students into teams of five, and distribute **Student Sheet 2.2, The Functions and Design Rationale of Telephone Components** and the old telephones if you have enough.

If each team has a telephone, they should disassemble it together in the same way the disassembly team did in Step Three. If there are not enough telephones, have students fill out **Student Sheet 2.2** using the telephone disassembled in Step Three.

To get students thinking about design issues, team members will answer another question about each telephone component: Why is this component designed the way it is?

In **Student Sheet 2.2**, students categorize the components by function using their completed grids from **Student Sheet 2.1**. Have students list the functions in the left column of **Student Sheet 2.2** and fill in the rest of the row with the parts that perform that function. Notice that some parts have more than one function.

Beyond the basic function of each part (e.g., sending, receiving), have students consider the design rationale based on each component's function. For example, a plastic cover is easy to clean and protects the inner components; a plastic handset cord is flexible and sturdy; and a circuit board uses a small amount of energy to transmit information. **Sample Student Sheet 2.2** on page 13 has examples of student answers.

Team members should work together to fill out their grids. You may wish to visit each team as they work to help students identify the parts of the telephone, and to ask leading questions to get students to broaden their thinking about design.

Allow about 30 minutes for students to disassemble the telephone and fill in the grid.

Sample Student Sheet 2.2

The Functions and Design Rationale of Telephone Components

Function	Component Design Rationale	Component Design Rationale	Component Design Rationale
Sending	**Microphone** To fit into a handset, to be sturdy, to pick up sound in the human vocal range	**Handset cord** To be flexible, to be sturdy, to be easy to clean, to be easy to replace	
Receiving	**Speaker** To fit into a handset, to be sturdy, to transmit sound in the human vocal range	**Handset cord** To be flexible, to be sturdy, to be easy to clean, to be easy to replace	
Energy input	**Wall cord** To be sturdy, to be easy to replace, to be safely insulated		
Structural support	**Screws** To hold other parts together easily and effectively	**Handset** To be easy to hold, to put the speaker and microphone in the right places	**Plastic cover** To protect components from dirt, moisture, etc.
Data entry	**Key Pad** To be easy to punch, to be easy to see, to transfer a lot of information in an easy way		
Controls	**Circuit board** To use a small amount of energy to transmit information, to allow the telephone to have features like redial	**Wiring** To efficiently transmit electricity and electrical impulses or messages	
Protection	**Plastic cover** To be sturdy, to be easy to clean		

Technological Advances

Telephone design has changed over time as a result of small and large inventions, advances in technology, and new uses. The first telephones, for example, transmitted electrical current over steel wires. When and why did this change to copper wire? When and why did fiber optic cables begin to be used? When and why did satellite transmission begin to be used? History, design, energy flow, environmental impact, and economics have played a role in each advance. Students should think of the telephone as transition technology, changing greatly in their lifetimes, and subject to advances in science and technology that they could personally influence.

Day Two

Step Five: Hold a discussion of each team's results and compile one master grid on the overhead projector or on a large sheet of butcher paper. Save this grid for the last unit of this book.

Emphasize that design plays an important role in determining the final form each component will take and the materials that compose it. But design is also a very important consideration in each step of the phone's life cycle. Tell the class that in the next four units they will closely examine these steps, and will develop some information as "experts" within their group that will help them evaluate the design of the phone of the future.

Step Six: Present the **Technological Advances** sidebar as an overhead. To fully investigate the life cycle of the telephone, each student in the team will consider each stage of the life cycle from one of five different perspectives (expert roles): history, design, energy flow, environmental impact, and economics.

Each of these perspectives is taken into consideration during a life cycle assessment. If your class is using *Life Cycle* in its entirety, this research will culminate in a class presentation and written report at the end of Unit Seven.

Hand out the **Student Sheet 2.3, Life Cycle of a Product—Expert Roles**. Each team member should choose a role. Have a short class discussion about the roles to make sure students understand what they are researching.

When students are clear about what their roles are, assign them—as homework or in the library—to do a literature search to better understand their roles. They should begin by gathering information about the telephone from reference sources such as encyclopedias or the Internet. As they study each of the following four units, they should record information they have learned in their lab journal and expand their literature search to include more specific information.

Require that they record their sources—paper- or Web-based—since students will revisit this information as they look at the other steps in a life cycle analysis. If students are new to this kind of research, you may want to involve your school librarian to help students with literature search methods. Require students to hand in a list of the resources they consulted as proof of their work.

Learning Goals

Unit Two has been constructed to guide student understanding of the following Learning Goals.

Enduring understandings

*   *Design requires taking constraints into account. These constraints include the properties of materials used, as well as economic, political, social, ethical, and aesthetic choices.*

*   *There are several ways to approach design problems.*

*   *Materials from human societies affect both the physical and chemical cycles of the Earth.*

Important facts and skills

*   *Each component of a telephone has its own design constraints, as does the final telephone.*

*   *Each product has a design history; its history influences what a product does and what it looks like.*

*   *Energy is one of the limiting factors of design.*

*   *Many people contribute to the design of any product, including the telephone.*

These Unit Two Learning Goals contribute to student learning of the following *National Science Education Standards* and *Benchmarks for Science Literacy.*

National Science Education Standards

Unifying Concepts and Processes
       Form and function
Science and Technology: Content Standard E
       Abilities of technological design
       Understandings about science and technology
Science in Personal and Social Perspectives: Content Standard F
       Environmental quality: Material from human societies affects both physical
       and chemical cycles of the Earth

Benchmarks for Science Literacy

3 The Nature of Technology
       3A Technology and science
       3B Design and systems
8 The Designed World
       8B Materials and manufacturing
       8D Communication

Resources

DESIGN

Publications

Andreu, J. 1995. *The Remanufacturing Process.* Design for Environment Research Group, Manchester, England: Manchester Metropolitan University. [also available at http://sun1.mpce.stu.mmu.ac.uk/pages/projects/dfe/pubs/dfe24/report24.htm]

Campbell, V., Lofstrom, J., and B. Jerome. 1997. *Decisions—Based on Science.* Arlington, Virginia: National Science Teachers Association.

Hardin, G. 1968. The tragedy of the commons. *Science.* 162:1243-1248.

World Commission on Environment and Development. 1987. *Our Common Future.* Oxford, England: Oxford University Press.

Young, J. E., and A. Sachs. 1994. *The Next Efficiency Revolution: Creating a Sustainable Materials Economy.* World Watch Institute Paper 121. Washington DC: World Watch Institute.

Web Sites

Design for the Environment Research Group, Guidelines: http://sun1.mpce.stu.mmu.ac.uk/pages/projects/dfe/guide/guidlin3.html

Hewlett-Packard, HP and the Environment: http://www.hp.com/abouthp/environment/

Nortel Networks, Lifecycle Management Solutions: http://www.nortelnetworks.com/corporate/community/habitat/lms/index.html

U.S. Department of Energy, Center of Excellence for Sustainable Development: http://www.sustainable.doe.gov/

U.S. Environmental Protection Agency, Design for the Environment: http://www.epa.gov/dfe/

U.S. Environmental Protection Agency, Environmentally Preferable Purchasing: http://www.epa.gov/opptintr/epp/

The World Bank Group, Development Education Program, Education for Sustainable Development: http://www.worldbank.org/depweb/

The Structure and Materials of a Telephone

Component	Function(s)	Structure (raw materials)
Microphone	Sending	Iron, plastic

Invention of the Telephone

Alexander Graham Bell (1847–1922) was an inquisitive and insightful inventor. Bell is known for the invention of the telephone, but he also worked on development of the first wax cylinder for the phonograph, invented a metal detector, and pioneered education for deaf students.

In 1874, Bell began work on an invention that would dramatically improve the use of the telegraph so that the telegraph could respond to many electrical impulses at the same time. In the spring of 1875, Bell, working with Thomas Watson, figured out that using a changing current to vary the resistance in a battery-powered circuit would conduct sound waves. Bell filed his telephone patent application in February of 1876, and it was issued in March. It has been called the most valuable single patent in history. Soon after his patent was issued, Bell mounted a platinum needle on the transmitter diaphragm. When the needle was dipped into a weak acid solution, the needle dipped and rose according to the strength of a current that passed through the needle, through water, and to an electromagnetic receiver. Bell noted the result and called to Watson through the mouthpiece, "Mr. Watson: Come here—I want you." Watson heard the message, responded, and the telephone was born.

The functions and Design Rationale of Telephone components

Function	Component Design Rationale	Component Design Rationale	Component Design Rationale
Sending	**Microphone** To fit into a handset, to be sturdy, to pick up sound in the human vocal range		

Life Cycle of a Product—Expert Roles

Life cycle assessment (LCA) originated in the early 1960s as workers tried to minimize the environmental impacts of products. Each stage in a product's life—design, raw materials, acquisition and processing, manufacture, useful life, and disposal—must meet the economic and environmental goals of society. However, the least expensive way to manufacture a product may not be the most environmentally friendly choice.

Each stage in the life cycle requires decisions, and these decisions require trade-offs. By considering each stage individually, you will learn the basics of how designers, engineers, manufacturers, and others use LCA to make desision about their products.

In designing a product, several factors guide the process. You should plan to research your role in the library or on the Internet to explore the importance of your role's impact on the design of a telephone. Your research goal is to become informed about your role and product, and to become an expert for your team.

"Bookmark" promising Web sites and record the reference books you use in your lab journal, because you may want to cite material or revisit these sources of information during future units in your exploration of life cycles. **Answer the questions for the role you have taken, recording your thinking in your lab journal.**

History

Your job is to take the long view—look at how history has led to the development of this product.

- What has been the impact of telephones on human communication? How did telephones change the way individuals and businesses operate in industrialized society?

- How have the raw materials, manufacture, use, and disposal of the telephone changed over time?

- Were there earlier designs of the telephone?

- Were there earlier products designed to accomplish the same function? If so, list them, and list the skills that may have been required to produce them.

- How has the design changed? Why?

- How have cell phones changed the way people communicate? Pagers? Beepers?

- How have computer modems impacted the way we shop, explore knowledge, and communicate?

Design

Your job is to look at how the design process works at each stage of the life cycle.
As this stage *is* design, you are focusing on how the design process itself is designed. The design of any product is usually a team effort.

- What may have been the skills of the people who developed the telephone? List the various kinds of abilities you think have contributed to its design.

- If the telephone looks to you as though it could benefit from additional expertise, list what you think it could use.

Energy Flow

Your job is to look at the energy considerations in each stage of the life cycle of the telephone. Each piece of this product needs energy to be built, shaped, polished, or processed to make it what it is. A key issue in any design is to minimize the energy expenditure wherever possible, to keep costs down, and to allow manufacturing plants to be built wherever shipping and distribution are efficient, not just where energy is cheap and plentiful.

- What energy inputs may have been planned during the design of the telephone?

- Can you suggest any changes in the telephone's design that may make it more energy efficient to produce?

Environmental Impact

Your job is to look at any environmental impact that may result from the production of the telephone. To keep costs down and environmental impact to a minimum, the design should make a product without generating too much solid, liquid, or gaseous waste that cannot be recycled into other products.

- Which components of your product probably generate waste that *can* be reused?

- Which components of your product probably generate waste that *cannot* be reused?

- Which stage of the life cycle of a telephone generates the most waste? Why?

- What can you suggest to make your product more environmentally friendly?

- Can you suggest any materials that could be substituted in your product design that would have less environmental impact?

Economics

Your job is to look at the economics of the total life cycle of the telephone. Each piece of the process costs *something:* labor, materials, production tools, disposing of waste in landfills (or reselling it as someone else's raw material), shipping, distribution, and packaging.

- Which parts of the life cycle of a telephone are the most expensive? Why?

- What components of the telephone are the most expensive?

- Are there less expensive materials that would work?

- What economic trade-offs may have been made in the design of this product?

- Can you suggest any design considerations that may lessen the cost of manufacturing, owning, packaging, shipping, or disposing of the product?

- What other industries have been influenced or created due to telephones?

Raw Materials— Acquisition and Processing

Summary

In the course of history, the use of various materials changes as a result of a complex set of factors: the depletion of some natural resources, new methods for processing materials, and changes in taste and fashion. When the United States was largely a nation of independent farmers, the predominant raw materials were those that required little modification from their natural state—slate and stone, cotton, wool, leather, grasses, and especially wood. Industrialization demanded materials that required more energy and new skills to process, such as metal alloys, reinforced concrete, and sheet rock. As the pace of industrialization quickened after the 1830s, Americans began to form more of their world from metals. Now, in the postindustrial age, many of our materials are synthesized from liquid and gaseous resources through chemical processes even more complex and energy-intensive.

Unit Three asks two questions about the telephone, and indirectly about all products: *What is it made of, and why?*

Objectives

- To examine the second stage in the life cycle— raw materials

- To use a literature search to explore various aspects of three of the main materials in a telephone: plastic, metals, and silicon chips

- To model the extraction of metal from ore, using a traditional laboratory activity

Time Management

Three or four class periods

Materials

- Plaster of Paris
- Sand
- Copper sulfate crystals
- Mortar and pestle or similar tools
- Tap water
- Clear, household ammonia solution
- Iron filings, iron powder, or iron nails
- Chalcopyrite
- Plastic spoon or stirring rod
- Graduated container
- Filter funnel and filter paper
- Beakers
- Dropper
- Two small test tubes
- Hand lens
- Safety goggles
- Safety apron

Preparation

If your class has just completed Unit Two, refer students to **Student Sheet 2.1, The Structure and Materials of a Telephone** and **Student Sheet 2.2, The Functions and Design Rationale of Telephone Components** for their initial materials analysis of the telephone parts. Students can visually revisit the partially disassembled telephone to provide a conceptual link for the raw materials analysis.

If your class has not recently done Unit Two, have groups of students examine and partially disassemble a telephone to prepare for Step Two of this unit (See Unit Two, Step Three). Exhaustive answers are not necessary.

At least one night before conducting the simulation activity (see Step Seven), obtain samples of chalcopyrite from a local rock and mineral supply source or through a scientific supply store. Prepare simulated copper ore with Plaster of Paris. Prepare 250 ml of liquid Plaster of Paris according to label directions and add two to three spoonfuls of coarse sand. As the mixture begins to thicken, stir in a spoonful of copper sulfate crystals to simulate the copper found in this ore. Allow the mixture to harden overnight and then break up pieces for each team to use. In this activity, the copper sulfate represents the copper mineral in an ore deposit.

Teaching Sequence

Day One
Step One: Review homework from Unit Two.

Step Two: Have students categorize the components of a telephone by the materials used in its production.

- Plastics
- Silicon chips
- Metals, including copper, iron, aluminum, lead, gold, and silver

Step Three: Have students consider the list from Step Two. Note that the materials listed as components of the telephone are not raw materials. With few exceptions, each material is itself the result of an acquisition process, a refining or processing process, and a manufacturing process. On an overhead, write "plastic parts" near the bottom, leaving plenty of space above to write steps that contribute to the acquisition of raw materials. On another overhead, write "metals." On a third, write "silicon chips." Address these major component materials in turn, using the following questions to start students thinking in this direction.

- What raw materials were needed to make this component of the telephone?
- What energy may have been used to make each?
- What byproducts may have also been produced in the production of each material?

As students answer these questions, represent their answers on the overhead, building a simple flowchart of processes and raw materials.

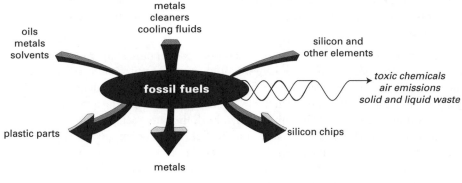

As the discussion progresses, ask students to suggest where they might turn to find out these answers. This is an opportunity for students to share the Web sites, books, and other sources they used for their individual literature search in Unit Two. Students should make notes about these sources in preparation for their individual literature search on raw materials.

Step Four: Assign **Student Sheet 3.1, Raw Materials—Expert Roles**, as homework. Using this handout, students explore the raw material of one of the three primary materials in a telephone—metals, plastic, or silicon chips. Divide the class into three teams, and assign each team one of the three materials to research. Within each team, assign one student to each of the five roles—history, design, energy flow, environmental impact, and economics. Adjust the role assignments if you have more or less than five students per team.

The handout provides background for each role, and provides example questions to ask and answer from each role's point of view. Have the teams meet briefly to share ideas about the assignment. Team members will then work on their own to answer the questions associated with their roles.

Day Two

Step Five: Begin class with a discussion of the homework. Class members circulate their findings and review their colleagues' work.

To summarize their findings, hold a class discussion of the origins of the three major materials. The summary discussion should afford team members an opportunity to present what they have learned verbally, and gives class members an opportunity to learn about all three materials. At the conclusion of this step, students should have a sense of the parallel paths of raw material acquisition and processing.

Assign **Student Sheet 3.2, Processing Copper from Chalcopyrite Ore** as a homework reading assignment to prepare for the lab on Day Three.

Day Three

Step Six: Present **Conservation of Mass and Atoms in a Chemical Reaction** sidebar as an overhead. Students should recall the Law of Conservation of Matter and the First and Second Laws of Thermodynamics from **Student Sheet 1.1**.

Conservation of Mass and Atoms in a Chemical Reaction

This activity is a good opportunity to emphasize that mass and atoms are always conserved in a chemical reaction. This is a simple, single displacement reaction:

$$CuSO_4 + Fe \longrightarrow FeSO_4 + Cu$$

Copper sulfate, Iron, Iron sulfate, Copper

In this case, the copper ions in solution react with iron. The iron acts as an oxidizing agent by giving up two electrons to the copper ion and reducing it to copper metal atoms:

$$Cu^{2+} (aq) + 2 e^- \longrightarrow Cu (s)$$
$$Fe (s) \longrightarrow Fe^{2+} (aq) + 2e^-$$

$$Cu^{2+} (aq) + Fe (s) \longrightarrow Cu (s) + Fe^{+2} (aq)$$

Ammonia can detect the copper ion in concentrations as small as one hundred parts per million (ppm). A simple and very sensitive test for copper uses ammonia (ammonium hydroxide) to form the dark blue-colored copper ammonium complex ion:

$$Cu^{2+} (aq) + 2 OH^- \longrightarrow Cu(OH)_2$$
(greenish-blue)

$$Cu(OH)_2 + 4 NH_3 \longrightarrow [Cu(NH_3)_4]^{2+} + 2 OH^-$$
(dark blue)

When the concentration of copper ions is high, the hydroxide ion in ammonia reacts with copper ions to form the greenish blue precipitate of copper hydroxide [$Cu(OH)_2$]. However, when the concentration of copper ions is low, the copper

continued on next page

Conservation of Mass and Atoms in a Chemical Reaction *continued*

hydroxide formed is readily converted to the blue tetra amine complex [Cu(NH$_3$)$_4$]$^{2+}$. This complex can be detected by the naked eye to a level of approximately 100 ppm and serves as a fairly sensitive test for the presence of copper ions in solution.

This activity relies on the tetra amine complex. Students will first check for c opper ions in a treated solution, then check for copper *leachates* (materials that seep out of mining residue) by adding water to the simulated *gangue* (the residue of worthless minerals in an ore deposit) in their filter paper.

Topic: mining

Go to: www.scilinks.org

Code: LCS01

Step Seven: Present **Lab Safety** sidebar as an overhead. Hand out **Student Sheet 3.3, Simulating Mining and Extraction of Copper from Ore.** This laboratory activity simulates the extraction and refining of copper from ore. Help students understand that this activity is not the same as the process described in **Student Sheet 3.2**, but in many ways models it.

Demonstrate the unique color of copper compounds and pure copper when heated. Place a small amount of copper sulfate solution on a nichrome or similar wire. Turn off the lights and place the wire in the flame of a bunsen burner. Students should notice the characteristic blue-green flame color. You can also produce the blue-green color by heating a copper wire. Point out that both the pure metal and its ions produce the same characteristic blue color. The field of emission spectroscopy is based on the fact that each element gives off a characteristic spectrum (bright lines) when heated. That spectrum can be used to identify the element and its concentration in the sample tested. Students will use this method to test whether they've succeeded in extracting copper from their simulated ore.

Step Eight: Distribute a small piece of simulated ore, and have students crush it. Everyone must wear eye protection when the "ore" is crushed. Ask students to compare the energy they use to crush their tiny piece of ore to the amount of energy needed to crush tons of ore, and note that real rock is harder than Plaster of Paris.

Step Nine: Have students perform the activity using the procedure in **Student Sheet 3.3.** Students use their simulated copper ore to model the separation and refining process. Their simulated ore contains the most commonly manufactured compound of copper: copper sulfate (CuSO$_4$).

Students use chemical extraction to refine the ore. With real copper ore, chemical extraction involves the addition of sulfuric acid to convert copper ores to copper sulfate. The copper sulfate solution is then electrolyzed to produce pure copper. In this activity, students replace the copper in solution with an inexpensive metal—iron. Emphasize that this reaction involves a single chemical displacement of iron for copper. This displacement process is not used in the actual refining process, but serves as a model for the actual process.

Assign the questions at the end of the student sheet as homework.

Day Four
Step Ten: Discuss the results of the simulation activity and the homework questions. Students should be able to note two signs of a chemical change. The first sign is the characteristic color of the solution that contained copper ions has changed from blue to a dull gray. The second sign is the change in energy: heat is given off in the reaction.

Review the answers to the questions. Questions 1–5 refer to knowledge students should have gained in their extraction simulation and from the reading. Questions 6–9 are designed to allow students to show that they can apply their knowledge. You may choose to use Questions 6–9 as class discussion questions.

Answers to Student Sheet 3.3
and Suggestions for Class Discussion

1. *Make a flowchart, like the one your teacher drew, to explain each step of the simulation activity and what you observed.*

   Flow diagrams will vary, but make sure all steps are included. Arrows should connect each step, and sidebars might indicate what tests were performed and what the results were.

2. *What evidence do you have that copper was present in the simulated ore?*

   The blue flakes or crystals in the simulated ore, the results of testing the water solution with ammonia, and the flame tests are evidence that there was copper in the simulated copper ore.

3. *Give evidence that a chemical change occurred when you added the iron to the blue-colored copper solution.*

   There are two signs that a chemical change occurred when students added the iron to the copper solution. The color of the solution changed, and there was a change in energy (i.e., heat was given off). Show students that there is a third sign of a chemical change. The iron forms a *precipitate*—a substance separated from a solution or suspension by a chemical or physical change.

4. *How could you prove to someone that the reddish-gold solid in your filter paper contained pure copper?*

   The flame test of the reddish-gold solid showed a bluish-green color, which is the characteristic flame test color of copper. Also, if the solid is pressed down with a knife blade, the solid shows the copper metallic sheen representative of copper.

5. *What are the next steps needed to refine your copper and change it into wire that can be used as part of the telephone cord?*

   Electrolytic reduction, milling

Answer the following questions from the point of view of your role.

6. *What waste was produced in this simulation? At what stages? Did the wastes contain harmful levels of copper? What is your evidence? What could you do to minimize this hazardous waste? Compare these wastes to the volume produced in the actual extraction and refining process described on **Student Sheet 3.2, Processing Copper from Chalcopyrite Ore**.*

   The wastes produced in the simulation are both solid and liquid in nature. In the first step, the filter paper contains a high concentration of copper ions in the liquid that adhere to solid gangue. As the water evaporates, high concentrations of coppper ions are left behind. In a more efficient process the solids would be washed thoroughly with water to reclaim any soluble copper ions, and then added to the next step of the process. The gangue (which is simulated by sand and Plaster of Paris) poses a significant disposal problem. These residues may be abandoned tailings piles or mounds that scar the landscape. In the second step of recovery, the copper has been removed from solution but now the solution contains a high concentration of iron both as a solid and as ion. The solid iron can be recycled back onto the process but the iron chloride solution must be treated as a waste.

7. *A sample of copper ore contains 0.5 percent copper metal. How much copper metal could be extracted from one ton of ore? (one ton = 907 kg) Assume refined copper sells for $2.50 per kilogram. If the cost of ore processing, extraction, and refining is $10.50 per ton, is it worthwhile to extract the copper in the ore?*

Lab Safety

Copper sulfate—like almost all copper compounds—is toxic! Avoid contact with the skin or eyes and immediately wash off any blue solution you spill on yourself. Dispose of the copper and the resulting iron sulfate in accordance with your school's policy for chemical waste disposal.

- Use precaution with copper sulfate solutions. *Copper sulfate is poisonous and an irritant.*

- Use ammonia in a well-ventilated room. *Never mix ammonium with a chlorine product.*

- *Always wear safety eyewear.*

One metric ton equals 1000 kilograms; 0.5 percent times 1000 kilograms equals 5 kilograms of pure copper. Therefore, the copper extracted would be worth 5 times $2.50 per kilogram or $12.50. Subtracting the cost of $10.50 per metric ton to process the ore leaves a profit of $2.00, making it marginally worthwhile to process the ore, unless part of the ore contains more than 0.5 percent copper. This problem shows students the need to analyze the relative advantages and disadvantages of a procedure as part of a decision-making process.

8 *What would you do with the solution that contains iron? What do you need to consider, for example, if the solution were dumped into a lake?*

This is a different question. Students may recognize that they could have to be careful when disposing of iron solution—that they couldn't dump it in a lake because it could harm fish or plants.

Explain that iron is normally benign in the environment since it easily reacts to form insoluble compounds in both soil and water. However, dumping iron into a confined body of water like a lake or pond could have deleterious effects because the iron may remove other valuable mineral nutrients from the water. The best solution for waste disposal is to concentrate the iron solution and either dispose of it or pass it on to another company which uses iron sulfate in one of its processes. Iron sulfate is used to make iron supplement tablets and also as a soil micronutrient fertilizer.

9 *In what ways did the simulation differ from the actual extraction process as described in **Student Sheet 3.2, Processing Copper from Chalcopyrite Ore**? In what ways is it similar?*

Answers will vary depending on the student role.

Learning Goals

Unit Three has been constructed to guide student understanding of the following Learning Goals.

Enduring understandings

- *Matter has characteristic properties, which are related to its composition and structure.*

- *Energy appears in different forms, and can move (be transferred) and change (be transformed).*

- *Interactions can produce changes in a system, although the total quantities of matter and energy remain unchanged.*

- *The raw materials for products are either removed from Earth or grown and harvested.*

- *Materials from human societies affect both the physical and chemical cycles of the Earth.*

Important facts and skills

- *Products can be defined and categorized by their raw materials, and by what happens to those raw materials.*

- *The four basic areas of life cycle assessment are: materials acquisition; manufacture and transportation; use and maintenance; recycling and waste disposal. Each step of the cycle involves understanding how energy, human impact, and waste production are part of a complex system.*

Microchips

Many students may not know that microchips in the telephone are made from an ultra-pure form of silicon. Silicon is the second most abundant element in the earth's crust. It occurs mainly in the form of silicates (compounds of silicon and oxygen, often combined with other metals such as aluminum, calcium, magnesium, and iron). The chips control dialing functions, number recall, and a wide variety of features, depending on the model of phone.

THE WORLD'S A CLICK AWAY

Topic: microchips

Go to: www.scilinks.org

Code: LCS05

These Unit Three Learning Goals contribute to student learning of the following *National Science Education Standards* and *Benchmarks for Science Literacy.*

National Science Education Standards

Physical Science: Content Standard B
      Structure and properties of matter
      Conservation of energy
      Interactions of energy and matter
Earth and Space Science: Content Standard D
      Geochemical cycles
Science in Personal and Social Perspectives: Content Standard F
      Natural resources
      Environmental quality: Material from human societies affects both physical
      and chemical cycles of the Earth

Benchmarks for Science Literacy

5 The Living Environment
      5E Flow of matter and energy
7 Human Society
      7E Social trade-offs
8 The Designed World
      8B Materials and manufacturing
11 Common Themes
      11B Models

Resources

METALS

Web Sites

The Copper Data Center: http://www.copper.org/

Innovations, How Do They Bring Copper to Market?
      http://innovations.copper.org/how/how01.htm

Mineral Information Institute: http://www.mii.org/

National Mining Association: http://www.nma.org/

PLASTICS

Publications

Lipscomb, R. 1997. *Polymer Chemistry, Revised Edition.* Arlington, Virginia: National
      Science Teachers Association.

Web Sites

American Plastics Council: http://www.plastics.org/

Australian Institute of Petroleum Education, Online Projects:
      http://www.aip.com.au/education/projects/

Calibre Plastics, Ltd., An Introduction to Plastics:
http://www.calibre.co.nz/plastics.htm

Plastics Resource (American Plastics Council's information on plastics and the
environment): http://www.plasticsresource.com/index.html

Shell Oil Company, The Crude and the Refined:
http://www.shell.com/royal-en/content/0,5028,25610-51252,00.html

ACID RAIN

Publications

Barracato, J. 2000. *Inside Rain: Working with Precipitation Chemistry Data.* Arlington,
Virginia: National Science Teachers Association.

Smith, P.S., and B.A. Ford. 1999. *Project Earth Science: Meteorology, Second Edition.*
Arlington, Virginia: National Science Teachers Association.

Web Sites

Resources for the Future, The Costs and Benefits of Reducing Acid Rain:
http://www.rff.org/disc_papers/summaries/9731.htm

U.S. Environmental Protection Agency, Acid Rain Program:
http://www.epa.gov/acidrain/

U.S. Geological Survey, Acid Rain Data and Reports:
http://bqs.usgs.gov/acidrain/

TOXIC WASTES

Publications

Barracato, J. 1998. *Toxics Release Inventory: Teacher's Guide.* Arlington, Virginia: National
Science Teachers Association.

Harr, J. 1996. *A Civil Action.* New York: Vintage Books.

Web Sites

U.S. Environmental Protection Agency and Agricultural & Biological Engineering
Department, Purdue University, Hazardous Products in the Home:
http://www.epa.gov/grtlakes/seahome/housewaste/house/mainmenu.htm

U.S. Environmental Protection Agency, Office of Solid Waste, Household Hazardous
Waste: http://www.epa.gov/epaoswer/non-hw/muncpl/reduce.htm#hhw

U. S. Environmental Protection Agency, Toxics Release Inventory:
http://www.epa.gov/tri/

Raw Materials— Expert Roles

The origins of any product are grown, harvested, and processed; or they are taken from the Earth and processed. The route between the beginning of a growing thing and its appearance in a product, or the first bucket full of earth and its appearance as a product, are stories on their own. **Follow these routes for the role you have taken, recording your thinking in your lab journal.** You should plan to read further in the library or on Web sites you've "bookmarked" from your telephone design work to answer your role questions for the raw materials for the telephone's plastics, silicon chips, or metals.

When you work with your team, you should be able to use your role's point of view to help your team describe the raw materials section of the life cycle of the telephone.

History

Raw materials have a history. **Your job is to take the long view—looking at the history of the use of the raw materials of a telephone.**

- What else has this raw material been used for?

- Does its historical use suggest why it was chosen for a telephone?

- Are there other raw materials that have been or could be used in a telephone?

Design

The process of making a material must be designed—with all the usual constraints of a design process. **Your job is to look at how the design process works at the raw materials stage.** Obtaining raw materials can have an impact on the environment unless the whole process is carefully designed. However, even in the most cautious design, trade-offs must be made.

- Where did the raw material originate?

- What technology was used to make it useable as a raw material?

Energy Flow

Your job is to look at the energy used to build the telephone. Each raw material of this product needed energy to be harvested, extracted, or refined. Energy is a key expense of any raw material. Aluminum, though a common element in the Earth's crust, was seldom used before a refining process was invented that took less energy. Glass requires relatively low temperatures to melt and process. Metals require high temperatures to melt and form, and large amounts of energy to separate and refine them from ore. The table on page 30 shows some comparisons.

- List the types of energy inputs that may have been needed during the harvesting or extraction of the raw material of a telephone.

Energy Needed to Produce Materials

Refined material	Typical product	Energy [in mega joules (MJs)] to produce 1 metric ton from raw materials
Glass	2 L bottle	12,960
Paper	large grocery bag	30,960
Copper	copper wire	134,100
PET plastic	grocery bag	86,040
Aluminum	soda can	178,380

- Consider other materials that you could substitute. Would any of them have lower energy requirements? Explain.

Environmental Impact

Your job is to look at any environmental impact that may result from the processing of raw materials for this product. The nature of this processing is to remove unwanted material, leaving a useable result. Examples of this processing range from the removal of seed coverings and other debris from wheat kernels to removal of seawater and unwanted ocean minerals to make table salt. The goal of any processing is to use the smallest amount of energy, and to generate the smallest amount of solid, liquid, or gaseous *byproducts* (products of an industrial or biological process in addition to the principal product) that cannot be recycled into other products.

- What is the environmental impact from use of the raw materials of your telephone?

- Can you suggest any materials that could be substituted in the making of the telephone that could have less harmful environmental impact?

Economics

Your job is to look at the real costs associated with the refinement and use of the raw materials chosen. Every step in the process costs something: acquisition, labor, land, unintended environmental consequences of the harvest or extraction, and disposing of byproducts (*e.g.*, plant parts). The raw materials that form plastic, copper, and silicon chips and the unattached plastic, copper, and silicon chips are "owned" by a succession of people or companies, and are sold each time the material changes hands. Each industry has trade journals that report on this process. You should be able to find these on the Web.

- Draw a chart of the various "owners" of the raw materials, from exploration through delivery of the refined raw material to the manufacturing plant.

- What is the ratio of raw material amount to refined material amount? For example, how does the amount of copper ore compare with the amount of refined copper? Add this to your chart.

- What ratio is needed for the refining company to make a profit? Consider the market price of refined copper versus the cost of ore processing.

- Give a rough accounting of money exchange at each step. Add this to your chart.

Processing Copper from Chalcopyrite Ore

People first began to use copper in its native, or elemental, form around 5000 BCE (before the Common Era) when they discovered accessible copper deposits. The soft copper could be formed into bands for jewelry or used to make cooking vessels. But pure copper is not rigid enough to be a sturdy knife or sword, and it was eventually discovered that mixing copper and tin produces a better material: bronze. This mixture of metals (called an *alloy*) could be used to create a wide variety of products, including weapons. The Bronze Age lasted from about 3000–1200 BCE.

Copper, gold, silver, and platinum are good conductors of heat and electricity. Because copper is fairly abundant and relatively inexpensive to refine, it is used extensively to transmit electricity.

Mining

Copper (chemical symbol: Cu) is extracted primarily from the mineral chalcopyrite ($CuFeS_2$), sometimes called copper pyrite. Copper is also found in these *ores* (minerals from which profitable metals can be extracted):

1. Azurite ($Cu_3[CO_3]_2[OH]_2$)

2. Bornite (CuS)

3. Chalcocite (Cu_2S)

4. Malachite ($Cu_2CO_3[OH]_2$)

Most copper ores, including chalcopyrite ore, contain an average of less than 0.5 percent copper. Separating this tiny percentage of copper from the 99.5 percent waste means that refining copper from this ore is a complex process—both in finding the metal and handling the waste. Chalcopyrite is mined from large open pits or underground mines that are sometimes enlarged at a rate of 1.8 million metric tons each week—that's 1,000,000 pickup-truckloads each week.

Crushing and Extraction

Once the chalcopyrite ore is hauled from the pit or mine, it is ground to a fine powder at a mill. The powder is mixed with water, oil, and a detergent. The detergent causes the copper and other valuable metal compounds in the ore (silver, gold, molybdenum, etc.) to form a bubbly froth that floats to the water's surface. The froth of concentrated ore is skimmed off the surface and dried. The other part of the powdered rock—called *tailing*—is discarded into a pond or a pile. Tailing is piled until it can be replaced into the pit or mine, or leveled and covered with layers of earth. Tailings from long ago can sometimes now be mined as ore—the invention of new extraction methods can remove minerals that the old methods missed.

Smelting

Concentrated ore is shipped to a smelter. After several runs through a furnace to burn off non-copper elements, the ore is combined with other materials and heated to separate out the copper and to drive off the sulfur. What remains is 99 percent pure molten copper called *blister*. The smelter captures the sulfur to sell, but also releases small amounts into the atmosphere. Atmospheric sulfur combines with oxygen to form sulfur dioxide ($Cu_2S + O_2 \longrightarrow 2Cu + SO_2$), which reacts first with a catalyst to produce sulfur trioxide (SO_3). Sulfur trioxide then reacts with water in the atmosphere, forming sulfuric acid ($SO_3 + H_2O \longrightarrow H_2SO_4$). Sulfuric acid is a primary component of acid rain, which can have devastating environmental effects.

Refining

The 99 percent pure copper produced in smelting is still not pure enough to be used for copper wire. The crude copper is again heated in a furnace to drive off combined oxygen and other impurities, then cast into a thin sheet called an *anode*. The copper anodes are placed in a solution of acid and copper sulfate. Positive and negative charges are applied to the copper anode in a process called *electrolytic reduction*. The copper anode dissolves to form positive copper ions, which are attracted to the cathode at the negative end and form a coating of 99.9 percent pure copper. Other impurities in the copper—gold, silver, platinum, etc.—fall to the bottom as the anode dissolves. These minerals are later recovered.

Manufacturing

The 99.9 percent pure copper can now be melted again and formed into rods, wires, sheets, tubes, and a variety of other shapes. In the United States, about 70 percent of the copper is used for electrical purposes (including telecommunications), 16 percent for construction, 6 percent for machinery, and 3 percent for the automotive industry (source: Copper Data Center). The main producers of smelted copper are the United States, Chile, Russia, and Zaire. Copper is roughly valued at $2,500 per metric ton; compared with iron at $350/ton, lead at $1,100/ton, aluminum at $1,600/ton, and gold at $10,000,000/ton.

Environmental Impacts of Mines

During operation of a mine, waste rock, dust, and liquid wastes (called *slurry*) can cause problems if not carefully contained. After a mine closes, waste heaps, mineshafts, or quarry pits may cause hazards and can spoil a landscape. Copper compounds, even in very low amounts such as a few parts per million, are toxic. These compounds have been used historically to rid pools of algae, kill plant life in drains, and keep marine life from growing on boat hulls. Water passing through mine dumps or old mines may dissolve and transport minerals to creeks and rivers. Sulfur dioxide and other gases emitted from mines cause air pollution. For all these reasons, the mining industry today is held to guidelines set by the EPA to reduce these threats to the environment.

Simulating Mining and Extraction of Copper from Ore

Background

Copper is used to carry energy from electrical generating plants to your home. This material is found in all appliances and computers, and in the communication device you use daily—the telephone. For these uses it must be extremely pure—99.9 percent pure—but first the copper must be mined and separated from ores.

In ore, copper is usually found in combination with other elements such as sulfur, oxygen, and iron. Rock is considered copper ore if at least 0.5 percent of it is copper. Copper processors separate copper from the other elements, then purify it. The residue left from purifying copper is mostly silica compounds that are not useful and must be disposed of as a waste. The finely ground residue (called *slurry*) may dissolve in rainwater (a process called *leaching*) and be carried to streams and lakes. The products of leached slurry are called *leachates*. The toxic material in leachates endangers the living things in the water. The leachate may also pose a threat to human drinking water supplies. In this activity, you will use a sensitive test to detect toxic copper residues and examine some ways to reduce these wastes in the environment.

Procedure

1. Read **Lab Safety** sidebar.

2. Obtain a sample of simulated copper ore from your teacher. If available, examine a sample of chalcopyrite, the most common copper ore. Use the hand lens to view the ore and **record the description in your lab journal.**

3. Carefully crush the simulated ore using a mortar and pestle. Place the crushed sample on a paper towel. Describe what you see now. Is this an example of a chemical or physical change?

4. Add the crushed material to a beaker and add 10 mL of water. Stir. **Record what you observe in your lab journal.**

5. Carefully filter the solution into another clean, dry beaker. Note the color. Examine the contents of the filter paper. Save the filter paper and residue for tests.

6. A simple test for the presence of copper in solution is to add a few drops of household ammonia to a solution suspected to contain copper. If the copper concentration is very high the resulting precipitate is greenish-blue. If the concentration is high, the color is greenish-blue or very dark blue, and as the concentration decreases the blue color will become gradually lighter.

Purpose

In this activity, you will model the extraction of copper from ore. You will also investigate some of the environmental impacts, waste disposal issues, energy expenditures, and economics that accompany the use of this product.

Materials

- Simulated copper ore
- Mortar and pestle or similar tools to grind the ore
- Tap water
- Clear, household ammonia solution
- Iron filings, iron powder, or iron nail
- Chalcopyrite
- Plastic spoon or stirring rod
- Filter funnel and filter paper
- Graduated container
- Beakers
- Dropper
- Two small test tubes
- Hand lens
- Safety eyewear

Lab Safety

Copper sulfate—like almost all copper compounds—is toxic! Wear safety goggles at all times, and avoid contact with the skin or eyes and immediately wash off any blue solution you spill on yourself. Ask your teacher to show you how to dispose of the copper and the resulting iron sulfate.

7. Remove a dropper full of solution from your beaker and place it in a test tube. Add five drops of ammonia solution and record the color in your lab journal. Add five drops of ammonia to the material in your filter paper. **Record your observations in your lab journal.**

8. Metals can be used to displace copper from its compound in a solution. That is, copper is removed from solution and replaced by another metal such as iron. Add a spoonful of iron powder to the blue-colored solution in your beaker. Stir and carefully observe any changes you see. Continue stirring until the color of the solution is no longer blue.

9. Filter the solution in your beaker into another clean, dry beaker. Use the spoon to remove the solid material and place it in the filter paper. Use some water to help remove residue, and let the water and residue drip onto the filter paper.

10. Use your dropper to remove a dropper full of solution from your beaker and place it in another clean, dry test tube. Add five drops of ammonia solution and **record the color in your lab journal.**

11. Elements produce different colors when heated. The *flame test* is commonly used to identify the presence of elements. Your teacher will use a Bunsen burner to test the blue solution, the colored solid in your filter paper, and the remaining solution you treated with iron. **Record the color of the flame and what this test tells you in your lab journal.**

12. Clean up and dispose of the materials as directed by your teacher.

Homework Questions

1. Make a flowchart, like the one your teacher drew, to explain each step of this simulation activity and what you observed.

2. What evidence do you have that copper was present in the simulated ore?

3. Give evidence that a chemical change occurred when you added the iron to the blue-colored copper solution.

4. How could you prove to someone that the reddish-gold solid in your filter paper contained copper?

5. What are the next steps needed to refine your copper and change it into wire that can be used as part of the telephone cord?

Answer the following questions from the point of view of your role.

6. What waste was produced in this simulation? At what stages? Did the wastes contain harmful levels of copper? What is your evidence? What could you do to minimize this hazardous waste? Compare these wastes to the volume produced in the actual extraction and refining process described on **Student Sheet 3.2, Processing Copper from Chalcopyrite Ore.**

7. A sample of copper ore contains 0.5 percent copper metal. How much copper metal could be extracted from one ton of ore? (one ton = 907 kg) Assume refined copper sells for $2.50 per kilogram. If the cost of ore processing, extraction, and refining is $10.50 per ton, is it worthwhile to extract the copper in the ore?

8. What would you do with the solution that contains iron? What do you need to consider, for example, if the solution were dumped into a lake?

9. In what ways did the simulation differ from the actual extraction process as described in **Student Sheet 3.2**? In what ways is it similar?

Manufacturing a Product

Summary

Manufacturing is the step in the life cycle that creates final products out of raw materials. Manufacturing begins with the initial receipt of raw materials and includes on-site storage, packaging, and distribution. In the manufacturing of a product, some new decisions must be made; for example, the product must be easy to assemble, the assembly must be easy to do over and over again, and waste must be minimal or easy to handle.

Objectives

- To make a protective package for a frozen dessert

- To consider materials and design options and weigh the energy, economic, and environmental impacts of the package

- To highlight the trade-offs and decision-making needed at each stage of the life cycle of a product

Preparation

This activity presents a simple design and manufacturing challenge. The results are then used to introduce a fairly sophisticated decision-making process.

Make uniform ice cubes (same size and volume) and put each ice cube in a resealable plastic bag. Each team will need at least one ice cube, so make extras. Keep ice cubes in a school freezer, and transport them to students in a cooler. Dry ice for the cooler is nice if you have it available, but be sure to use mitts and be careful as you handle it. Have materials (aluminum foil, paper, plastic wrap, tape, etc.) ready for students who do not bring their own.

Time Management

Four class periods

Materials

- Heat lamp
- Balances
- Cooler with dry ice or block ice
- Ice cubes
- Plastic zipper-style sandwich bags
- Aluminum foil
- Cardboard
- Felt or cloth
- Wax paper
- Plastic wrap
- Newspaper
- White office paper
- Clear tape
- Duct tape
- Masking tape
- Paper clips
- 50 mL graduated cylinders
- Timer or stopwatch
- Small trays

Teaching Sequence

Day One

Step One: Introduce the third stage in the life cycle of a product—manufacturing. In a short class discussion, invite students to list the types of issues that are important to consider in the design and maintenance of a manufacturing process.

Tell students that next class period they will design a manufacturing process for a frozen dessert wrapper. Have students meet in their teams, and hand out **Student Sheet 4.1, Test Sheet: Chill Out!** Have the teams answer questions 1–4 together. These questions help them identify the goal of their package. Based on this goal, students weigh different design options in order to determine which materials make the most effective frozen dessert wrapper.

There is no "right" answer. Students can use any materials they think will work, but must consider the relative effectiveness of different materials. Is a paper wrapper as effective as a plastic wrapper? Why? Have students bring in materials to construct the package for the ice cube. The **Materials** section lists possible materials, but is not an exhaustive list.

Hold a discussion with the class to determine their knowledge of what insulators are and how they work. Develop the concept that an insulating material prevents the flow of heat from an area with a higher temperature to an area of lower temperature. This is called the Second Law of Thermodynamics. Recall from Unit One that when energy is changed from one form to another, some of the useful energy is always degraded to lower-quality, more-dispersed, less-useful energy (You can't break even).

Develop the idea of heat flow in the wrapper. Because energy always moves from an area of more energy to an area of less energy, heat will always flow into the wrapper. The wrapper's job as an insulating material is to prevent this process from happening too quickly. Insulators work because they are made of materials that trap air (air is a poor conductor of heat) or slow heat flow. Have students discuss this idea in their teams and begin to consider the insulating value of the materials they will select to make the wrapper.

Day Two

Step Two: Working in their teams, students design and build a frozen dessert wrapper by creating a package that keeps ice cubes from melting. Allow students just 20 minutes to complete their design and construction. If necessary, you may need to remind students that it is *only* a frozen dessert wrapper, not something complicated like a telephone.

When students finish building their wrapper prototype, hand out **Student Sheet 4.2, Design Rationale Form** for students to complete.

Step Three: Review the testing procedure with the whole class, since many of the steps are time-sensitive. Each team now tests their wrappers and gathers information about the effectiveness of their design.

When teams finish their wrappers, distribute ice cubes in the plastic bags. Students quickly find the mass of the bag and cube. Students then put the plastic bag with the ice cube into the team's wrapper, and place the package on the small tray under the light, as described on **Student Sheet 4.1**. Time exactly 15 minutes.

After 15 minutes, teams quickly open the wrapper and plastic bag, and measure how much water has melted, using the graduated cylinder. If any water leaks from the package, it will collect in the tray. Students should include the leaked water in the graduated cylinder measurement. Students weigh the cube in the plastic bag and calculate what percent of its original mass remains. If time allows, teams can repeat the melting process with another ice cube to get an average measurement for their wrapper.

Assign **Student Sheet 4.3, Post-Build Questions** for homework or for completion during the 15-minute waiting period.

Day Three

Step Four: Review the homework. After a discussion on design criteria your class will reach a consensus on which is the best wrapper.

Have the class look at the steps on the **Design Rationale Form**. Have them develop a list of design criteria to evaluate the wrapper (some suggestions are: history, energy requirements, environmental impact, and cost) and melt test results (effectiveness).

Lead the class through a discussion and a procedure to decide which design criterion is most important. As a class, rank the importance of the wrapper design criteria on a scale of 1 to 5, with 5 representing the most important criterion and 1 the least. This rating system gives the most important criterion the most weight when students analyze individual wrappers in the next step.

___History of wrappers.

___Energy required in manufacturing this wrapper.

___What environmental impacts will this wrapper have—either during manufacture or after the product is shipped?

___How much money do you think you will need to charge for this wrapper?

___How well does the wrapper work?

Step Five: Once the attributes have their importance ranking, have the class consider another aspect of decision-making: analysis. Have the class consider how each team's wrapper performed in each design category. For example, if a wrapper design uses little energy, assign it a favorable rating (5). If a wrapper uses materials or a process that had major environmental impacts, assign it an unfavorable rating (1). Develop a chart to display each team's wrapper ratings. Enter the rankings and the ratings.

By assigning an importance ranking to each criterion (cost, effectiveness, etc.), the most important criterion will have the most weight when all of the factors are considered. For example, if the class determines the most important criterion to be the environmental impact of the wrapper (ranking = 5), an environmentally friendly wrapper (rating = 5) should out-perform a wasteful wrapper (rating = 1), even if the wasteful wrapper costs less.

SCI LINKS
THE WORLD'S A CLICK AWAY

Topic: raw materials

Go to: www.scilinks.org

Code: LCS0

For each team's wrapper, multiply the rankings times the ratings and enter that value in the "Ranking x Rating" column. Then, find the total for each group's wrapper by finding the sum of each Ranking x Rating column.

Ranking	Group 1		Group 2		Group 3		Group 4	
	Rating	Ranking x Rating	Rating	Ranking x Rating	Rating	Ranking x Rating	Rating	Ranking x Rating
1. ——								
2. ——								
3. ——								
4. ——								
5. ——								
	Total		Total		Total		Total	

Analyze the data collected. Which wrapper has the best overall rating? The wrapper with the best overall rating goes into mass production!

Day Four

Step Six: In this step, a group tries repetitive manufacture of the selected wrapper.

Present *Assembly Lines* sidebar as an overhead for discussion. Assemble sufficient raw materials for the leading wrapper design to make five copies of the prototype. Have a team that did not build the highest rated wrapper begin the manufacturing process for the wrapper. If students want to build their own design instead, remind them that those who engineer a design are seldom the same people who manufacture a product. This points out two things: division of labor and the importance of communication between designers and builders.

Give the manufacturing team 20 minutes to build five copies in front of the class, following the instructions written by the prototype designers. This should be a fun task. The point of the exercise is to show that the most successful product can still encounter pitfalls in the manufacturing process. If there are manufacturing problems, how can they be addressed? Is it still possible that one of the other prototype designs would have had a more successful manufacturing process?

Step Seven: Hand out **Student Sheet 4.4, Manufacture of a Food Wrapper—Expert Roles**. There are two ways to use this handout to conduct this wrapper wrap-up:

1. Use the handout questions as a guide to reemphasize points that you feel students might need to revisit based on your review of the teams' **Design Rationale Forms.**

2. Regroup the role players of each team into an all-design team, an all-environmental impact team, etc. Give the new teams the handouts, have them answer their role questions, and then have each new team present their summary of the issues raised in the questions to the class.

After either method, ask each team to consider how they would redesign the package in light of this discussion. Can students think of examples of products they use that may have had a good initial design, but were not manufactured well? (Almost any product, from food to pencils to telephones to cars has this potential problem!)

If time permits, students can manufacture and test the redesigned package.

Assign each group a one- to two-page paper to synthesize what they have learned from the roles handout and use this as an evaluation of the unit. Give students two nights to complete the paper, allowing time to meet with their group members.

Step Eight: In all stages of a product's life cycle, the transport of materials is an important consideration. For example, raw materials must be moved from mines to mills and then shipped to fabricators where they are incorporated into other products that may become the subcomponents of a finished product. Manufacturing plants are usually located near ports, railroads, or major highways. Have students consider the energy used by boats, trains, and trucks during transport. Students should also realize that the energy inputs (work, fuel) and the resulting wastes generated by transportation (e.g., airborne gases) must be considered in any life cycle assessment.

Optional: Assign students a short research project for homework. Students can pick a heat-sensitive product (ice cream, frozen dinner) and research its distribution from plant to grocery store. Most major companies have Web sites, to which students can refer. Have students write a short, one- to two-page, paper on their research findings.

Learning Goals

Unit Four has been constructed to guide student understanding of the following Learning Goals.

Enduring understandings

- *Technology is an integral part of science.*

- *Costs, risks, benefits, and other human aspects of a problem are important considerations.*

- *Energy plays a role in every transformation of matter.*

- *Mass remains the same in phase changes of matter.*

Important facts and skills

- *Many viewpoints contribute to successful understanding.*

- *Many aspects of science play a role in successful design.*

- *Social issues influence science and technology.*

- *Science concepts offer effective decision-making tools.*

Worth being familiar with

- *History shapes our current understanding of science and technology .*

- *Materials have various abilities to insulate.*

Assembly Lines

The manufacturing process owes a great debt to Henry Ford (1863-1947), an American industrialist who revolutionized factory production. In 1908, Ford began selling the Model T car, which at that time was manufactured by workers one car at a time. Public demand for these cars was so great that Ford was forced to find a faster way of manufacturing.

Ford studied meat-packing houses and grain conveyors, and developed an ingenious solution. Ford created an assembly line in which workers installed just one part of a car as the car traveled past on a moving conveyor belt. The assembly line, which can be found in every factory today, allows workers to focus on performing one task very well, rather than performing a variety of tasks.

These Unit Four Learning Goals contribute to student learning of the following *National Science Education Standards* and *Benchmarks for Science Literacy*.

National Science Education Standards

Unifying Concepts and Processes
    Form and function
Science and Technology: Content Standard E
    Abilities of technological design
    Understandings about science and technology
Science in Personal and Social Perspectives: Content Standard F
    Environmental quality: Material from human societies affects both physical
    and chemical cycles of the Earth

Benchmarks for Science Literacy

3 The Nature of Technology
    3A Technology and science
    3B Design and systems
8 The Designed World
    8B Materials and manufacturing

Resources

MANUFACTURING

Web Sites

AT&T, Resources for Educators, Fiber Optics:
    http://www.att.com/technology/forstudents/brainspin/fiberoptics/

Fiber Optic Test Equipment Company, Fiber U Online Lesson Plans:
    http://www.fotec.com/fiberu-online/fuonline.htm

Intel, How Microchips Are Built: http://www.intel.com/education/chips/

The Primary Sources Network, Manufacturing Units:
    http://primarysources.msu.edu/curricula/lessons/manu/

PACKAGING

Publications

Wisconsin Department of Natural Resources. 1993. *Recycling Study Guide.* Wisconsin
    Department of Natural Resources, Education Section. Publ-IE-020 93 Rev.

Web Sites

Aseptic Packaging Council: http://www.aseptic.org/

Test Sheet: Chill Out!

Background

The delicate electronic components inside a telephone are protected from dust and spills by a plastic case. In this activity, you will manufacture a package to solve a similar problem—how to protect the contents of a package from the outside environment. Your challenge is to design a package that keeps an ice cube from melting. You can use any materials you think are necessary (the materials list has some suggestions). Each team will test its wrapper with an ice cube contained in a small, resealable plastic sandwich bag.

Before you build and test your package, complete the following. **Record your answers in your lab journal.**

1. What is the function of your ice cube package?

2. Which materials will you use for your package? Why?

3. How will these materials help achieve the function of the package?

4. Sketch your design. (Your design may change once you begin building, but this initial step will help you plan your wrapper.)

Purpose

To design and manufacture an insulating package that is economically efficient and environmentally friendly.

Procedure

1. Bring necessary materials to class. Your teacher will provide ice cubes and plastic bags.

2. Build your ice cube package. You will have about 20 minutes to do this.

3. Fill out your team's **Student Sheet 4.2, Design Rationale Form**, which asks you questions about why you chose the materials and design you did. **Record your answers in your lab journal.**

4. When you receive your ice cube, quickly find its mass (while it's in the plastic bag) and **record this starting mass in your lab journal.**

5. Immediately after recording the mass, place the plastic bag containing the ice cube in your package, and position the package under a heat lamp or in a warm area. Wait exactly 15 minutes.

6. During the 15 minutes, **make notes on two or three of the other groups' designs (materials used, shape, size, etc.) in your lab journal.** From what you have discussed about insulators, and the Second Law of Thermodynamics, predict how well each will do to insulate the ice cube.

7. After 15 minutes, open the package and pour the melted water from the plastic bag into a graduated cylinder. Record the amount of water that has melted. Find the mass of the plastic bag and ice cube, and record the ending mass.

8. Calculate the % of the mass of the ice cube lost. Repeat the test as time allows.
   [(Starting Mass − Ending Mass)/Starting mass] x 100 = % of Mass Lost

9. Complete the data table below. (You may only have time for one trial.)

	Starting Mass (g)	Ending Mass (g)	Mass Lost (Percent)	Melted Water (mL)	Mass Difference (g)
Trial 1					
Trial 2					
Average					

10. Post your Average results for "Mass Lost" and "Melted Water" for the class to see.

11. **Record your classmates' results next to your own in your lab journal.**

12. Post your team's **Design Rationale Form.**

13. Complete **Student Sheet 4.3, Post-Build Questions** for homework. **Record your answers in your lab journal.**

Design Rationale Form

1. Sketch the wrapper.

2. List the materials used.

3. List the steps to manufacture the wrapper. Describe the steps clearly enough so that a person unfamiliar with your team's wrapper could come in and build it using only your instructions. Someone will have to follow these instructions later in the unit.

4. Did you use a certain kind of wrapper as a model (e.g., plastic, paper)?

5. What energy will be required in manufacturing this wrapper?

6. What environmental impacts will this wrapper have—either during manufacture or after the product is shipped and used?

7. How much money do you think you will need to charge for this wrapper?

Post-Build Questions

1. After obtaining your results, account for the differences in your % mass loss and other groups' % mass loss.

2. From your results and what you have learned, how would you modify the design of your wrapper to try to improve its insulating value?

3. If you had to make 10,000 wrappers per day, describe the manufacturing process and how you would deal with increased waste and energy demands.

Manufacture of a food Wrapper— Expert Roles

Research your assigned role and then discuss the results with your group. Your assignment is to write a one- to two-page paper that synthesizes what you have learned in this activity and from the group's research on the manufacture of wrappers.

History

Your job is to take the long view—looking at how history has led to the food wrapper being manufactured the way it is.

- What has traditionally been used to insulate food and keep it sanitary?

- What were the constraints that package designers had 50 years ago or 100 years ago, when they set out to wrap food?

- Why were some packages more successful than others?

Your answers might include how strong the package was, how impermeable it was to water, how well the materials insulated the ice cube, how they absorbed or reflected light, or how they acted as conductors of thermal energy.

Design

Your job is to investigate how the manufacturing stage of the life cycle is designed. The package's design—which includes both the materials used and the construction— determines the effectiveness of the package. Compare your wrapper with those built by other groups.

- Why were some packages more successful than others?

- What common characteristics do effective packages share?

Your answers might include how strong the package was, how impermeable it was to water, how well the materials insulated the ice cube, how they absorbed or reflected light, or how they acted as conductors of thermal energy.

Energy Flow

Your job is to look at the energy required to manufacture the wrapper.

- Did making your wrapper require a lot of work (energy) from your group?

- How do the packages compare in terms of energy use?

For example, aluminum is a material that reflects heat well, but is expensive and takes a lot of energy to acquire and produce. Paper, on the other hand, is inexpensive, but it is a poor insulator.

Environmental Impact

Your job is to look at any environmental impact that may result from the manufacture of the wrapper. Consider what will ultimately happen to the materials your colleagues have chosen.

- Which materials can be recycled?

- Which materials are easily degraded and which are not?

- How can the amount of materials in the package be reduced so that less waste is created?

There are also energy considerations in the collection of the packages, in reprocessing packages into paper, and in sanitation. What are the trade-offs between glass vs. plastic beverage bottles (wrappers for liquid)?

Economics

Your job is to look at the economics of the manufacturing stage. Essentially, you are looking at what things cost.

- Does the manufacturing process take a lot of time, labor, or materials? Which of these three costs the most?

- Does it cost more to produce the product than you can make in selling it?

- Are there practical considerations that a manufacturing process must meet?

- What are the pros and cons of the economic costs of disposable and reusable containers?

A single-use product avoids contamination because after it is used once, it is thrown out, generating waste. A multiple-use product must be cleaned and disinfected, which also generates waste. In either case, any materials used must be sanitary and bacteria-free. This kind of practical consideration translates into unavoidable expenses.

The Useful Life of a Product

Summary

This unit explores the concept of the useful life of a common product. Students examine issues of durability, depreciation, and waste as they evaluate this part of a product's life cycle. The fourth stage in a product's life cycle is the actual use of that product by a consumer. This part of life cycle assessment, understanding the actual use and repair of products, is perhaps the least documented. Students can conduct original research by following the useful life of the common products used in their homes.

Objectives

- To explore the concept of the useful life of a common product

- To examine issues of durability, depreciation, and waste

- To use math and economics concepts to illustrate the useful life of a common product

- Optional: To conduct original research by following the useful life of the common products at home

Time Management

Two class periods

Materials

- A telephone that has ended its useful life
- Pencils
- Paper cup
- *Life Cycle of a Pencil* poster
- T-shirt

Preparation

The fourth stage in a product's life cycle is its actual use by a consumer. Once the consumer buys or makes a product, its useful life starts. There are costs and trade-offs at this stage also, with repair, maintenance, and energy use of the product. Useful life is everything that happens to a product between the time it is purchased and when it is thrown away.

Give students a copy of **Student Sheet 5.1, The Useful Lives of a Telephone and a Paper Cup—Expert Roles** to read for homework in preparation for this unit.

Before class begins, place several objects, including a telephone and a paper cup on a table where students can clearly see them. Display the *Life Cycle of a Pencil* poster.

Teaching Sequence

Day One

Step One: Hold up a paper cup and a telephone, and ask students to estimate how long each of these products would last before being either discarded or recycled. Clearly, the phone can be used many times for the same purpose, but the cup will be used once or twice and then discarded. Ask students to consider why this is so, and ask them for some differences in the manufacture and use of a paper cup and a telephone. (Briefly add plastic cups and glasses to the discussion if students need a continuum to start their thinking.)

Bring out through discussion that the nature of the materials and how those materials will be used determines the longevity of the product. The paper cup is manufactured from low-quality paper and only uses a few materials. The telephone, on the other hand, uses more expensive raw materials and takes more time to manufacture but will last longer. Present material from the **Effects of Design and Manufacture on Useful Life** sidebar as an overhead for discussion.

Step Two: Refer to the *Life Cycle of a Pencil* poster to point out where "Useful Life" falls in the life cycle. Ask the class members to describe what they've studied in the preceding units on Raw Materials and Manufacturing. Students should bring up several of the impacts and role inputs that have been studied and described during earlier units.

Ask: "If the useful life is the point of the whole product, what affects the product's useful life?" This is your segue into reviewing the homework reading. Draw students' attention to the four stages of the useful life: use, cleaning, repair, reuse, and perhaps donation. Ask for student volunteers to briefly describe the useful lives of the items on the table at the front. Students will investigate these four stages, primarily through the use of math and economics, for the next half class period and the following day.

Day Two

Step Three: Distribute copies of **Student Sheet 5.2, Useful Lives Comparison**. Use this handout to extend student thinking about the life cycle beyond the idea of a telephone, and to consider how trade-offs are made at this stage, as compared to other stages in the life cycle. Give students 15 minutes of class time to work alone to answer the handout questions, then discuss the answers as a class.

Step Four: Divide students into teams of five. These may be the same teams they've worked with in previous units, though they will not be required to play their role in this unit. During this step, students will calculate the monetary value of a telephone and a T-shirt.

Distribute **Student Sheet 5.3, Lives of a Product**. Students should discuss and answer the questions in teams. Students may need to be reminded that the wear and tear on a T-shirt or telephone varies, and what one person considers moderate use may be high for another. Allow 30 minutes for the teams to develop their answers. Randomly call on teams to provide an answer to the handout questions.

To give students additional context for these calculations, ask why certain cars are worth more than others after several years of use.

Optional Research Activity

This activity allows students to conduct an independent investigation on the useful life of a classroom telephone. Students will research where the school acquires its telephones, what the school does with the phones when they break, and how the school disposes of the phones.

Distribute **Student Sheet 5.4, Optional Research Activity—The Life of Your School's Telephones**. Split students into pairs and ask students to read over the goals of the activity and carefully plan their investigations before beginning research.

After students complete their research, have students write a short report for a homework assignment. You may wish students to present their reports. Lead a class discussion on their results, including what the school does with a telephone after they no longer use it. This will provide a transition to waste disposal, the topic of the next unit.

Effects of Design and Manufacture on Useful Life

The design and manufacture of a product affect its useful life. The original design of a product determines what materials will be used, and how the manufacturing process will operate. Inexpensive materials and poor manufacturing quality will result in a product with a short useful life. In turn, materials and manufacturing affect price, another determining factor of a product's useful life. A cheap product is easily discarded and replaced, and its low price doesn't create the incentive to repair and reuse that product. Why should a consumer reuse a paper cup when she can use a new one for very little cost? Paper cups can be manufactured cheaply with simple materials that aren't intended to last a long time because a paper cup is a *single-use product*—intended to be used once and thrown away. A glass cup is more expensive and has to be more durable, because it is meant to be reused.

Design also affects product durability in more subtle ways. The original design may have included modular components that can be easily upgraded or repaired individually. For example, a telephone cord is easily replaced, so you don't have to replace the entire telephone when the cord frays. All the prior stages of a product's life cycle—design, raw material acquisition, manufacturing, packaging, distribution—affect other stages, and ultimately that

continued on next page

Answers to Student Sheets and Suggestions for Class Discussion

Effects of Design and Manufacture on Useful Life
continued

product's useful life. To extend the lifetime of a product, design should take into account aesthetic qualities. Many still-useful products quickly go out of fashion and are discarded in favor of more stylish ones.

Student Sheet 5.2

1. *For each of the products listed below, estimate its useful life. Then discuss your estimates with other members of your group and arrive at a group consensus for each item.*

   Answers will vary; most students will probably say the washing machine or toaster has the longest useful life.

2. *What product had the shortest useful life? Why?*

   Answers will vary, but most students will probably say that the paper cup or the foam cup has the shortest useful life. You might want to use this to start a discussion on the advantages of a paper cup over a polystyrene foam cup.

3. *Pick three products and explain how you could extend their useful life.*

   Answers will vary. Depending on the product, some ways to extend a product's useful life are to repair it when it breaks, patch holes, keep it in good working order, clean it, and donate it if you are no longer using it.

4. *Use some of the products above to explain the advantages and disadvantages of having a very short useful life.*

   A product with a short useful life is probably cheap, simple to design and manufacture, uses a small number of raw materials, and has a small volume so it takes up minimal space in a landfill. However, a product with a short useful life is also likely to be thrown away without an attempt at repair or reuse, and thus contributes to the volume of the solid waste stream, encouraging the acquisition of more raw materials.

5. *Which products in the table do you think will use the most energy during their life? Give examples of energy uses for these products. Consider the energy they use while in operation, and the energy used to maintain them in a good working condition.*

   Answers will vary, but students will probably say that a washing machine uses the most amount of energy during its life. Washing machines require energy to spin clothes, heat water, and (for some machines) provide power for an electronic display. Other products that use energy are the toaster and portable CD player (which use energy only while in operation), and the cell phone and cordless phone (which use energy all the time).

6. *Which product in the table generates the most waste during its life? Consider electricity use, cleaning, and repairing.*

Answers will vary, but most students will probably say that a washing machine generates the most waste during its life. Not only does the electricity it relies on generate greenhouse gases, but the wastewater and soap byproducts can be detrimental to the environment. Since a washing machine has a long useful life, it will probably be cleaned several times, a process that generates waste (and regular household cleaners can be especially harmful to the environment). Since a washing machine is an expensive item, it is likely to be repaired rather than quickly replaced if it breaks. Repairing will also generate a small amount of waste, in the electricity used to run the tools that repair it.

7. *Because a product is inexpensive, does it make sense to use it once and then throw it away?*

Answers will vary. The purpose of this question is to get students thinking about trade-offs.

Student Sheet 5.3

1. *How does the price of a product change over time? Let's say you bought a T-shirt, wore it once, then sold it to a friend. Assume you paid $20 for the shirt. How much would you charge the friend after two days? After two weeks? After six months? After one year? After two years? What factors affected your decision?*

Answers will vary, but will show a declining price over time.

2. *After what period of time would you consider the T-shirt to have no monetary value? Why?*

Answers will vary.

3. *Now think about the monetary value of a more complicated product—the telephone. Assume you paid $75 for a regular cordless phone, used it once, then sold it to a friend. How much would you sell the phone for after two days? After two weeks? After six months? After one year? After two years? Graph your answers in your lab journal.*

Answers will vary, but will show a declining price over time.

4. *Is there a difference between the rate of decline in the price of a T-shirt and the price of a phone? Explain the price difference.*

Answers will vary, but the price of a telephone will probably decline much more rapidly than the price of a T-shirt.

Telephone History

1876: Alexander Graham Bell transmits his voice through a liquid telephone.

1896: The dial telephone is invented.

1921: AT&T begins manufacturing dial systems.

1954: The desk telephone is available in a range of colors, marking the first time the phone is used as a decorative item.

1964: The touch-tone telephone is introduced to consumers. Pushbuttons replace dials and clicks, allowing faster calling.

1984: The first portable cellular telephone is sold.

5. *How does technology affect the price difference? Consider a cellular phone: Will it have the same decline in price as a regular cordless phone? Explain any price differences.*

    Advances in technology cause the price of a product to decline rapidly. For instance, when cellular phones were first sold, they cost hundreds of dollars. Cell phones now cost about $80 (often including phone service) and will likely cost even less within a few years as new advances in technology develop and cell phones become easier to manufacture. The resale cost of a cell phone will also decline rapidly as older cell phones become obsolete. The price of a standard wired phone has remained roughly the same for the past several years, and will not change that much if resold.

6. *Calculate what the dollar value of a $75 telephone would be after one year, two years, and three years of use. Assume that a telephone depreciates at a rate of 20 percent each year. Graph your answers in your lab journal.*

    After one year, a $75 telephone will have a value of $60. After two years, that $75 phone will have a value of $48. After three years, the phone will have a value of $38.40. Discuss the graph.

7. *In the examples above, depreciation is used to calculate worth in economic terms. But does this mean that a phone will be not useful in three years, or that an older computer can't be used for any purpose at all? List 10 appliances in your home. How old are those appliances, and are they still useful?*

    Answers will vary.

Learning Goals

Unit Five has been constructed to guide student understanding of the following Learning Goals.

Enduring understandings

*   *Energy plays a role in every transformation of matter.*

*   *Science often advances with the introduction of new technologies.*

*   *Science and technology can help solve global challenges.*

*   *Human populations use resources in the environment to maintain and improve their existence.*

Important facts and skills

*   *Social and economic issues influence science and technology.*

*   *Science and math concepts are effective decision-making tools.*

*   *Graphing*

Worth being familiar with

*   *Earth does not have infinite resources.*

*   *Human consumption places stress on the natural processes that renew some resources, and it depletes those resources that cannot be renewed.*

These Unit Five Learning Goals contribute to student learning of the following *National Science Education Standards* and *Benchmarks for Science Literacy.*

National Science Education Standards

Unifying Concepts and Processes
       Systems, order, and organization
       Constancy, change, and measurement
       Form and function
Science in Personal and Social Perspectives: Content Standard F
       Natural resources
       Environmental quality: Material from human societies affects both physical and chemical cycles of the Earth
History and Nature of Science: Content Standard G
       Historical perspectives

Benchmarks for Science Literacy

7 Human Society
       7E Political and economic systems
8 The Designed World
       8B Materials and manufacturing
11 Common Themes
       11C Constancy and change

Resources

USEFUL LIFE

Publications

Durning, A. 1992. *How Much is Enough? The Consumer Society and the Future of the Earth.* Washington, DC: World Watch Institute.

Ryan, J. C., and A. T. Durning. 1997. *Stuff: The Secret Life of Everyday Things.* Seattle: Northwest Environment Watch.

GREENHOUSE GASES, GLOBAL WARMING, AND CLIMATE CHANGE

Publications

Education Department, Stephen Birch Aquarium-Museum. 1996. *Forecasting the Future: Exploring Evidence for Global Climate Change.* Arlington, Virginia: National Science Teachers Association.

National Energy Education Development Project. 1998. *Secondary Energy Infobook.* Herndon, Virginia: National Energy Education Development Project.

National Science Teachers Association. 1999. *Investigating Air.* Arlington, Virginia: National Science Teachers Association.

Stevens, W. K. 1999. Thinning sea ice stokes debate on climate debate. *New York Times.* November 17.

Warrick, J. 2000. Global warming is 'real,' report finds. *Washington Post.* January 13.

Web Sites

CSIRO Australia, Division of Atmospheric Research:
http://www.dar.csiro.au/info/material/info98_2.htm

Intergovernmental Panel on Climate Change: http://www.ipcc.ch/

National Oceanic and Atmospheric Administration,
Global Warming Frequently Asked Questions, July 20, 1998:
http://www.ncdc.noaa.gov/ol/climate/globalwarming.html

U.S. Department of Energy, Energy Information Administration,
Greenhouse Gases, Global Climate Change, and Energy:
http://www.eia.doe.gov/oiaf/1605/ggccebro/chapter1bak.htm

U.S. Environmental Protection Agency, Global Warming:
http://www.epa.gov/globalwarming/

The Useful Lives of a Telephone and a Paper Cup— Expert Roles

Directions

Read the information below to start your thinking about what affects the useful life of a telephone.

History

Consider the length of the useful life of a telephone. Trends and technology can affect how long the telephone is used. A rotary phone from the 1950s may still work, but it is not as desirable as a touch-tone or a cordless phone. Soon even cordless phones may be obsolete as society turns to cellular phones.

Design

The original design of a product determines what materials will be used, and how the manufacturing process will operate. In turn, materials and manufacturing affect price, another determining factor of a product's useful life. Less expensive products are easily discarded and replaced. A low price doesn't create the incentive to repair and reuse that product. Why should a consumer reuse a paper cup when a new one costs almost nothing? Paper cups can be manufactured cheaply with simple materials that aren't intended to last a long time because a paper cup is a *single-use product*, intended to be used once and thrown away. A glass cup is more expensive: it is meant to be reused and its materials and manufacturing must be durable.

The design may include modular components that can easily be upgraded or repaired individually. For example, a telephone cord is easily replaced, so you don't need to replace the entire telephone when the cord wears out. Design must also account for the attractiveness of a telephone, which makes people want to use it, and its functionality, which makes the telephone easy to use.

Energy Flow and Environmental Impact

A telephone—like other electric appliances—uses energy during its useful life. Phones with liquid crystal displays (LCDs), cordless phones, and phones with answering machines use additional energy. When considering energy use during the useful life of a product, remember not only the total consumption of energy, but also the greenhouse gases produced in power generation. Cleaning, repair, and maintenance also require energy, but their impact is primarily in the amount of waste products they generate. A paper cup may require no energy during use; a glass cup will be washed and dried.

Economics

Companies may make more money if they sell more products, so products may not be designed to last for years. If a product is part of a technology that is rapidly changing, as are telephones or computers, technology may make a product obsolete before the structural parts wear out. If a telephone is still usable, though out of date, it may be possible to sell or donate it, extending its useful life. Broken telephones may be repaired or recycled, but many more may end up in landfills.

Useful Lives Comparison

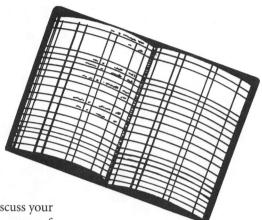

1. For each of the products listed below, estimate its useful life. Then discuss your estimates with other members of your group and arrive at a group consensus for each item.

Name of Item	Individual's Useful Life Estimate	Group's Useful Life Estimate
Cell phone		
Cordless phone		
Paper cup		
T-shirt		
Ballpoint pen		
Toaster		
Washing machine		
Sock		
Carpet		
Bicycle		
Portable CD player		
Polystyrene foam cup		

2. Which product had the shortest useful life? Why?

3. Pick three products and explain how you could extend their useful life.

4. Use some of the products above to explain the advantages and disadvantages of having a very short useful life.

5. Which products in the table do you think will use the most energy during their life? Give examples of energy uses for these products. Consider the energy they use while in operation, and the energy used to maintain them in a good working condition.

6. Which product in the table generates the most waste during its life? Consider electricity use, cleaning, and repairing.

7. Because a product is inexpensive, does it make sense to use it once and then throw it away? Explain your answer.

Lives of a Product

1. How does the price of a product change over time? Let's say you bought a T-shirt, wore it once, then sold it to a friend. Assume you paid $20 for the shirt. How much would you charge the friend after two days? After two weeks? After six months? After one year? After two years? What factors affected your decision?

2. After what period of time would you consider the T-shirt to have no monetary value? Why?

3. Now think about the monetary value of a more complicated product—the telephone. Assume you paid $75 for a regular cordless phone, used it once, then sold it to a friend. How much would you sell the phone for after two days? After two weeks? After six months? After one year? After two years? Graph your answers in your lab journal.

4. Is there a difference between the rate of decline in the price of a T-shirt and the price of a phone? Explain the price difference.

5. How does technology affect the price difference? Consider a cellular phone: Will it have the same decline in price as a regular cordless phone? Explain any price differences.

6. Calculate what the dollar value of a $75 telephone would be after one year, two years, and three years of use. Assume that a telephone depreciates at a rate of 20 percent each year. Graph your answers in your lab journal.

7. In the examples above, depreciation is used to calculate worth in economic terms. But does this mean that a phone will be not useful in three years or that an older computer can't be used for any purpose at all? List 10 appliances in your home. How old are those appliances, and are they still useful?

Optional Research Activity— The Life of Your School's Telephones

Purpose

You will investigate the useful life of a telephone in your school.

Procedure

1. Working in pairs, come up with questions you want to answer about the useful life of a school telephone. Some questions to consider are:

   - Was the phone manufactured in the United States? If not, where was it manufactured?

   - Where did the school buy the telephone?

   - Was the phone new when the school bought it?

   - How much did the phone cost?

   - How long does the school usually keep a telephone?

   - How often is a phone cleaned?

   - What is used to clean a phone?

   - What does the school do with the phone when it breaks?

   - What does the school do with a phone when it is no longer useful? For instance, does the school donate the phone to charity?

   - When the phone no longer works at all, does the school give the phone back to the phone company, recycle the phone, or throw it out?

   Think of other questions to find out about the life of a phone at your school.

2. Make a list of school faculty and administrators who may be able to help you answer these questions.

3. Talk to your sources, keeping careful notes on the information they give you.

4. For homework, write a two- to three-page report describing the useful life of a telephone in your school. Include a list of sources.

A Tale of Two Cups—Disposal and Reuse

Summary

What happens to a product when it no longer works and its useful life is over? The last stage in a product's life cycle is disposal or reuse—called the *end-of-life stage*. Students examine the trade-offs involved in selecting one drinking cup over another. They investigate what would happen to each type of cup as waste, and review the concept of life cycles as a way to consider waste management issues. Students then analyze the end-of-life stage for a telephone and explore what happens to each component of a phone.

Objectives

- To investigate the end-of-life stage of a product

- To examine the relative advantages and disadvantages of paper cups versus polystyrene cups

Preparation

Obtain enough polystyrene foam cups and paper cups (cups should have the same capacity) to give one of each type to every student in the class. Have enough rulers available for each student.

The final part of Unit Six asks students to research *municipal solid waste* (MSW) in their region. You can use these final questions in class or as a homework assignment. If your class has access to the Internet, bookmark two pages on the United States Environmental Protection Agency's *Municipal Solid Waste Factbook* Web site:

*   State MSW Data
    http://www.epa.gov/epaoswer/non-hw/muncpl/factbook/internet/mswf/states.htm#top

*   Individual State Profiles
    http://www.epa.gov/epaoswer/non-hw/muncpl/factbook/internet/mswf/prof.htm#top

If your class does not have Internet access, save the *Factbook* on the hard drive of your classroom computer(s) using instructions from the *MSW Factbook* Web site at http://www.epa.gov/epaoswer/non-hw/muncpl/factbook/. You may also print out the relevant data for your state from the State MSW Data and the Individual State Profiles Web sites shown above.

You will also need to do some advance research on the telephone system your school uses. As an alternative, have students use their own phones from home and contact the manufacturer using the Web to do their research. Have the telephones from Unit Two available for students to weigh.

Assign **Student Handout 6.1, Disposal** as a homework reading assignment the day before this class meets.

Teaching Sequence

Day One

Step One: Review homework from Unit Five.

Step Two: Divide students into groups of five and distribute a copy of **Student Sheet 6.2, A Tale of Two Cups** to each student. Distribute paper and foam cups to each group, and ask students to write a quick answer to Question 1 on **Student Sheet 6.2**. Take a vote to see how many students initially pick a foam cup, and how many pick a paper cup. Students may think that the foam cup is more harmful to the environment because the foam cup won't decompose. Explain that you are going to consider the impacts of each cup in more depth.

Step Three: Introduce the end-of-life stage in the life cycle of a product. Have students define municipal solid waste (garbage or trash), and give some statistics for the MSW stream in the United States. Introduce two end-of-life options for a product that reduce the amount of material in the MSW stream—composting and recycling. Composting is not a possibility for paper and foam cups, but both cups can be recycled in many areas.

Ask students to answer Question 2 on **Student Sheet 6.2**, and then review the answers. You may want to write a list on the blackboard to analyze the materials in each cup. The foam cup is molded of just one material, polystyrene. The paper cup has a plastic or wax coating inside to keep the liquid from leaking out. The paper cup also uses a glue to attach the sides to the bottom.

Time Management

Three class periods

Materials

*   Polystyrene foam cups (6–8 oz.)
*   Paper cups (6–8 oz.)
*   Rulers
*   Balances
*   Telephones from Unit Two
*   United States Environmental Protection Agency's *Municipal Solid Waste Factbook* (see **Preparation**, at right, for accessing the *Factbook* on the Web)

In Unit Two, the class dissected a telephone and saw that it is made out of many components. Unit Four showed students the complexity of manufacturing a product that is made out of many parts. The more complicated a product, the more complicated its end-of-life issues.

Ask students about the problems associated with recycling a product made of many different materials, such as the paper cup or a telephone. Help students recognize that the more raw materials in a product, the more energy and labor are needed to separate it and then recycle the different components. The cost of this labor and energy are what realistically determine whether there will be a market for the recycled product. The labor and energy costs also determine the market for a homogeneous product like a foam cup, which also must be cleaned, shredded, and reprocessed into another material. However, homogeneous products require less energy, labor, and money to recycle, and the shorter recycling process will generate less waste than a heterogeneous product like a paper cup.

The environmental effects of both cups during their life cycle also must be considered. Although the United States has the technology to recycle both cups, only foam cups are recyclable and are actually recycled in only a few communities. After the discussion on recycling, ask students to answer Question 3 on **Student Sheet 6.2**.

Step Four: Lead a short discussion on landfills and call on students to explain how they work. Ask students to answer Questions 4–6 on **Student Sheet 6.2**, and review their answers. These questions model the effect of landfilling solid waste. Since a landfill's capacity is determined not by the weight of materials deposited, but by its ultimate volume, students must consider the space occupied by each cup. Students begin to estimate landfill volume by using the heels of their shoes to compress the cups. Describe how landfills compress waste materials using consecutive layers of weight.

Students will see that the foam cup has a greater volume because of the airspaces in the foam that make it a good insulator. Question 5 asks students to reconsider their decision on which cup to use based on total landfill space occupied by each cup.

Step Five: Discuss the final option for the end-of-life stage of a product, incineration. Call on students to describe what incineration is and how it works. Consider incineration for a paper cup and a foam cup, and ask students to think about how much the volume of each would be reduced if the cups were incinerated. Paper cups leave more ash behind, because of their total weight compared to plastic cups. They also are made up of many kinds of different molecules compared to the one long polystyrene polymer molecule in the plastic cup.

Discuss the environmental hazards of incineration and focus on the byproducts of burning a paper cup and a foam cup.

Now consider one of the environmental benefits of incineration: energy conservation in a waste-to-energy incinerator. Explain to your class how a modern incinerator can harness and reuse the energy it generates from burning solid waste. Discuss energy release for the two kinds of cups. Ask students to reconsider their cup choice if the cups were to be incinerated, and have them answer Question 7.

Have students answer Questions 8–14 for a homework assignment.

Cup Incineration

In their Life Cycle Assessment (LCA), Franklin and Associates, LTD (1990) found that if combusted in an incinerator, foam cups release 46 percent less atmospheric emissions and 42 percent less waterborne wastes (wastes disposed of in water such as rivers and into groundwater) than paper cups. A pound of foam releases about twice as much energy as a pound of paperboard does when incinerated. However, a paper cup weighs slightly more than a foam cup of the same volume (a 16 oz paper cup weighs roughly 10.4 g compared to the 4.4 g of a 16 oz. foam cup). Thus, one paper cup has a greater potential for energy release than one foam cup, but the paper cup leaves more ash behind to dispose of in a landfill. The LCA on the two kinds of cups conducted by Franklin and Associates, LTD found that paperboard cups occupy 34 to 46 percent less landfill space than an equal number of polystyrene cups. Because polystyrene breaks down very slowly, few leachates are produced. Each disposal method involves the expenditure of energy, and the potential for harmful environmental emissions to land, air, and water is great. Therefore, each community must make the decision to use a particular method, and must consider where a recycling or disposal facility should be located.

Day Two

Step Six: Questions 8–13 use the data in Tables 6.1 and 6.2 to analyze energy use and savings in the life cycle of paperboard and polystyrene foam. Question 14 asks students to investigate MSW disposal options in their own region, using EPA's *Municipal Solid Waste Factbook*. Review the answers to these questions in class. Help students understand that each person has different values and priorities in the decision-making process, and there is no right answer as to which cup to choose. In Question 14, students may also consider whether the cup is made out of a renewable natural resource. The wood used to make paper is renewable; the petroleum that produces polystyrene is not renewable. Some students may also factor in the economic cost of the cup, and the cup's insulating abilities. Take a final vote on the student choices of cups and compare to the original vote.

Step Seven: Handout a copy of **Student Sheet 6.3**. Ask students if they have any old telephones stored in their homes. Are they still usable? Why haven't they been discarded in the trash? Bring out the concept that we tend to hold onto things we value—that still have monetary value—and don't discard them. Have them discuss what may happen in the future to these phones. Have students answer Student Question 1.

Step Eight: Have students look at their list of the phone's components from **Unit Two**, **Student Sheet 2.1**. Help them to estimate the rough percentages of plastics and metals in the phone. A starting assumption is that the phone contains 50 percent of each. Have the groups complete the activity.

As students complete the activity, check with the groups to see if each person has been assigned one of the four choices for further research in Student Question 3. Set a reasonable amount of time for them to research this and then report back to the entire class. Discuss the answers to Questions 1-3

Day Three

Step Nine: The highlight of this activity will come from each group's reports. This is an important time to point out the strengths of doing reports with more than one group member responsible for a single area. You may wish to have students in each small group work with members of other groups who are doing the same part of the research to pool their knowledge for the class report.

Step Ten: As a way to evaluate student learning in this set of activities, have students refer back to your discussion of single-use products that are fairly homogeneous like the cups. Have students consider these questions: What if single use products were banned? What information would they need to consider the implications of using a cup that could be reused many times, such as glass? How would you evaluate a glass cup? What environmental and energy considerations must be balanced in order to make a wise and sustainable solution about glass containers? Because both energy and material are now relatively inexpensive, we have a throw-away economy. But for how long? Is this sustainable? Will we someday be mining the landfills and other waste dumps for materials that may in the future become expensive and very scarce? What are the alternatives? How does life cycle analysis help us examine these alternatives? How can we consider the design of a product as a prime driving force to make all aspects of its life cycle more sustainable? This is the subject of the concluding activity of this book.

Answers to Student Sheets and Suggestions for Class Discussion

Student Sheet 6.2

1. *If you had to choose between a foam cup and a paper cup of equal size to use once and then throw away, which cup would you choose and why?*

    Answers will vary.

Recycling

2. *Look carefully at the paper and foam cups. List the materials that make up each cup:*

    Paper Cup
    Paperboard
    Plastic/wax coating
    Glue

    Foam Cup
    Polystyrene foam

3. *Which cup is physically easier to recycle, and why? Ignore what is actually recycled in your community.*

    The foam cup is easier to recycle because it is made out of only one material. The three different materials in the paper cup must be separated before they can be processed at a recycling facility.

Landfills

4. *Estimate how many paper and foam cups you use in a typical week. Remember to include cups used in your school cafeteria, fast food restaurants, movies, convenience stores, and at home. Then multiply each estimate by 52 to calculate the number of cups you use in a year. Show your calculations.*

    Answers will vary.

5. *Use the heel of your shoe to compress each cup as much as possible. Measure the dimensions and then calculate the volume of each cup. Multiply the volume of each cup by the estimated number of cups used in one year. Show your calculations.*

    Answers will vary, but will show that the volume of a compressed foam cup is greater than the volume of a compressed paper cup.

6. *What do the final answers of Question 5 represent? Based on those calculations, which cup would you choose if you were considering landfill space?*

    The final answers found in Question 5 represent the total volume occupied in a landfill by all the cups a student uses in one year. If landfill space were the only consideration, one should choose a paper cup, which—in great quantities—takes up significantly less space than a foam cup.

Incineration

7. *Using the data in Tables 6.1 and 6.2, explain why recycling materials into new products requires less energy than acquiring and processing virgin raw materials.*

    For almost all materials, recycling is more energy efficient than acquiring and processing virgin raw materials. Another waste disposal option, incineration, generates energy when material is burned. The second column in Table 6.2 represents the energy in mega joules (MJs) saved by recycling a ton of material rather than harvesting a ton of virgin material. The third column represents the amount of energy (in MJs) generated when one ton of that material is inciner-ated. The last column in Table 6.2 represents the ratio of energy savings from recycling compared to energy generated in incineration. This ratio is calculated by dividing the number of MJs/ton saved in recycling a material by the energy generated through incineration of that same material.

What is a Joule?

The joule is named after James Prescott Joule, a 19th-century British physicist. A joule is the standard metric measurement unit for work and energy.

8. *What do the second and third columns in Table 6.2 represent, and how are those values measured? What does the last column mean, and how is that value calculated?*

Material	Energy Saved by Recycling (MJ/ton) *	Energy Generated During Incineration (MJ/ton)	Relative Savings
Paper (other)	21,213	7,600	2.8:1
PET[1] plastic	85,888	21,004	4.1:1

[1] polyethylene terephalate
* Note: To covert to metric tons, multiply the number of tons by 0.907185

The second column is the energy saved through recycling. The third column shows the total energy generated by incineration. They are both measured in mega joules per ton of material. The last column is calculated by dividing the value of the second by the value of the third column to obtain this ratio. Recycling paper saves almost 3 times more energy than can be gained by incinerating it.

9. *What does Table 6.2 say about recycling vs. incinerating paper, and recycling vs. incinerating plastic?*

Incinerating one ton of paper generates 7,600 MJ of energy. Recycling paper saves 21,213 MJ, which is 2.8 times more energy than incineration generates. Incinerating one ton of plastic generates 21,004 MJ of energy. Recycling polyethylene terephalate (PET) saves 85,888 MJ, which is 4.1 times more energy than incinerating generates.

10. *Combine the data in the two tables to discuss overall energy use and savings for acquiring and disposing of paper and polyethylene terephalate (PET).*

The important consideration in using this question is an assessment of student decision-making. Students who respond with more than a single answer and compare and contrast the energy values, and what they have learned about waste management, will have been able to synthesize well the ideas of this activity. If energy is the only consideration, then the incineration of plastic cups is preferable to landfilling them. Recycling them would save 4.1 times more energy than incinerating generates. Recycling paper saves almost 3 times as much energy as incinerating it. See the answers in the previous question, which students can incorporate into their answer above. If the energy used in the acquisition of raw materials, their transportation and processing into a finished product, is the only consideration, then recycling saves a great deal of energy. Recycling one ton of paper uses 21,213 MJ less than acquiring and processing one ton of paper from virgin timber (34,400 – 13,187). Recycling one ton of PET plastic uses 85,888 MJ less than acquiring and processing one ton of PET from virgin petroleum (95,600 – 9,712).

Conclusions

11. *Your paper cup is made of paperboard, which fits into the "Other paper" category in Table 6.2. Your foam cup is made of polystyrene, which is very similar to PET plastic. If you use a foam cup, how should you dispose of it? If you use a paper cup, how should you dispose of it? Give numbers to support your answer.*

Again recycling wins over incineration or landfill disposal where no energy will ever be gained back from the cup. Students should incorporate some of the reasoning from the last two questions. In addition, they should draw upon the fact that paper takes up more room in a landfill than plastic. They should use numbers from their data in compressing the two cups to support this answer. In reality, it is landfill volume, not area, that ultimately determines the lifetime capacity of a landfill. If landfill area is at a premium, then volume becomes an important consideration.

12. *Having analyzed all the end-of-life options for foam cups and paper cups, choose one cup that you would use and specify the most environmentally friendly way to dispose of it. Explain your reasoning.*

Answers will vary.

13. *Given the regional statistics from EPA's Municipal Solid Waste Factbook, which cup will you choose to use? Explain your reasoning. Your choice may include other factors that are unrelated to the end-of-life stage of a cup's life cycle.*

Answers will vary.

Student Sheet 6.3

1. *What are some end-of-life options for a used telephone?*

Use this question as a way to review the options discussed in this activity. Make a list on the board of each option and what students consider to be each one's strengths and weaknesses. Call their attention to the fact that people store many old phones. Discuss the concept of value from the Teacher Background Information and extend this to a discussion of used computers.

2. *Give a rough estimate of how long the components (use broad categories) of your phone would last in a landfill using the chart below as a guideline:*

Banana/orange peel	2–5 weeks
Leather	1 year
Newspaper	up to 50 years
Aluminum can	80–100 years
Plastic bottle	100–200 years
Glass bottle	1,000,000 years

Students should be able to use aluminum as a rough estimate for the metals and the plastic PET bottle for the plastics. Point out that the chips are made mainly of silicon, the principal element found in glass.

3. *As a group select one person to:*

  * *Research on the World Wide Web the company that produced your phone. Find out what they consider to be the useful life for their phone and what their policy might be in accepting these phones back for recycling.*

  * *Contact your school's business office and research what kind of phone system is used in your school. Find out how long they think it will be useful and what is usually done with the system when it is replaced.*

- *Contact a local recycling center and ask them if they accept old phones. Contact a metals salvage dealer to see what you can learn about their recycling practices and what they know about the fate of old telephones.*

- *Contact your local waste management agency/company and ask them what their policy is regarding discarded telephones.*

After you have done your research, write a one- to two-page report to share with your group. Include who you contacted, the date, and what information you obtained. Then, discuss whether you consider your findings to be a good choice for the end-of-life for the telephone.

Answers will vary.

4. *Write a one-page article for your local newspaper that summarizes the results of your group's research and give your recommendations for what should be done with old telephones.*

Answers will vary.

Learning Goals

Unit Six has been constructed to guide student understanding of the following Learning Goals.

Enduring understandings

- *Matter has characteristic properties, which are related to its composition and structure.*

- *Energy appears in different forms, and can move (be transferred) and change (be transformed).*

- *Interactions can produce changes in a system, although the total quantities of matter and energy remain unchanged.*

- *Materials from human societies affect both the physical and chemical cycles of the Earth.*

Important facts and skills

- *The five basic areas of life cycle assessment are: design; materials acquisition; manufacture and transportation; use and maintenance; recycling and waste disposal.*

- *Each step of the cycle involves understanding how energy, human impact, and waste production are part of a complex system.*

These Unit Six Learning Goals contribute to student learning of the following *National Science Education Standards* and *Benchmarks for Science Literacy*.

National Science Education Standards

Physical Science: Content Standard B
      Structure and properties of matter
      Interactions of energy and matter
Life Science: Content Standard C
      Matter, energy, and organization in living systems
Science and Technology: Content Standard E
      Abilities of technological design
      Understandings about science and technology
Science in Personal and Social Perspectives: Content Standard F
      Natural resources
      Environmental quality: Material from human societies affects both physical
      and chemical cycles of the Earth
      Science and technology in local, national, and global challenges

Benchmarks for Science Literacy

3 The Nature of Technology
      3A Technology and science
      3B Design and systems
8 The Designed World
      8B Materials and manufacturing
      8D Communication

Resources

MUNICIPAL SOLID WASTE

Publications

Colborn, T., Dumanoski, D., and J. P. Meyers. 1996. *Our Stolen Future: Are We Threatening Our Fertility, Intelligence, and Survival?* New York: Dutton.

Franklin and Associates, LTD. 1990. *Resource and Environmental Profile Analysis of Foam Polystyrene and Bleached Paper Board Containers.* Prepared for the Council for Solid Waste Solutions. Washington, DC.

Hocking, M. B. 1991. Paper vs. polystyrene: a complex choice. *Science* 251:504–505.

McNulty, K. 1990. Bag it: the grocery sack dilemma. *Science World* 20 (April): 11–17.

Nolan, A. J., ed. 1999. *Understanding Garbage and Our Environment.* Middletown, Ohio: Terrific Science Press.

Rathje, W., and C. Murphy. 1992. *Rubbish! The Archaeology of Garbage.* New York: HarperCollins.

Ray D. L., and L.R. Guzzo. 1992. *Trashing the Planet: How Science Can Help Us Deal With Acid Rain, Depletion of the Ozone, and Nuclear Waste (Among Other Things).* New York: HarperPerennial.

United States Environmental Protection Agency. 1996. Characterization of Municipal
    Solid Waste in the United States, 1996 Update. Prepared by Franklin
    Associates, Ltd. for EPA. Washington, DC. EPA 530/R-00-024. [also available
    at http://www.epa.gov/epaoswer/non-hw/muncpl/msw99.htm]

Web Sites

United States Environmental Protection Agency's *Municipal Solid Waste Factbook:*
    http://www.epa.gov/factbook/internet/

Environmental Systems of American, Inc., Solid Waste Factoids:
    http://envirosysteminc.com/trash.html

RECYCLING

Publications

Booth, W. 2000. Recycling: how long will a can-do feeling last? *The Washington Post.*
    January 5.

Web Sites

The Aluminum Association, Recycling: http://www.aluminum.org/default.cfm/0/4/

American Forest & Paper Association, Paper and Wood Recycling:
    http://205.197.9.134/recycling/recycling.html

California Department of Conservation, Recycle Rex Education:
    http://www.consrv.ca.gov/dor/edu/

The Copper Page, Recycling of Copper:
    http://environment.copper.org/uk/ukrecyc.htm

Shop Recycled: A Consumer's Guide to Recycled Plastics:
    http://sourcebook.plasticsresource.com/mall/index.html

Steel Recycling Institute: http://www.recycle-steel.org/

Treecycle™ Recycled Paper, Issues and Information:
    http://www.treecycle.com/info.html

United States Environmental Protection Agency, Recycle City (an interactive game):
    http://www.epa.gov/students/recyclecity.htm

RECLAIMING

Publications

Goldberg, C. 1998. Where do computers go when they die? *The New York Times* March 12.

Mathews H. S., et al. 1997. *Disposition and End-of-Life Options for Personal Computers.*
    Green Design Initiative Technical Report #97-10. Carnegie Mellon University.

Parks, B. 1997. After life—where computers go to die. *Wired Magazine* Issue 5.07 (July).
    [also available at http://www.wired.com/wired/5.07/afterlife.html]

Pepper, I. L., C. P. Gerba, M. L. Brusseau. 1996. *Pollution Science.* San Diego:
    Academic Press, Inc.

Web Sites

British Telecom, Telephone Recycling:
http://www.bt.co.uk/World/environment/phones.htm

Innovation, New Life for Old Boards:
http://innovations.copper.org/199902/newlife01.htm

Republic Metals Corporation (a virtual tour of the Republic Metals plant):
http://www.republicmetalscorp.com/rmcslide/

COMPOSTING

Web Sites

Compost Resource Page: http://www.oldgrowth.org/compost/

The Digital Composter: http://www.digitalseed.com/composter/

Environmental Defense Fund, Composting in the Schools:
http://www.edf.org/heap/a_compost/index.html

United States Environmental Protection Agency, Composting:
http://www.epa.gov/compost/index.htm

LANDFILLS

Publications

Montague, P. 1989. Analyzing why all landfills leak. *Rachel's Environment and Health Weekly* #116 (February 14). [also available at http://www.rachel.org/]

———. 1991. Toxic gases emitted from landfills. *Rachel's Environment and Health Weekly* #226 (March 27). [also available at http://www.rachel.org/]

Web Sites

Environmental Industry Interactive, Professional Managed Landfills:
http://www.envasns.org/eii/garbage/landfills/landfills.htm

Enviroweb, The Basics of Landfills: http://www.enviroweb.org/issues/landfills/

United States Environmental Protection Agency, Landfill Methane Outreach Program:
http://www.epa.gov/lmop/

INCINERATION

Publications

Kopel, D. B. 1993. Burning mad: the controversy over treatment of hazardous waste in incinerators, boilers, and industrial furnaces. *The Environmental Law Reporter* 23 (April):10216–27. [also available at http://www.i2i.org/suptdocs/Enviro/ipincine.htm]

Morris, J. and D. Canzeroni. 1992. *Recycling Versus Incineration: An Energy Conservation Analysis*. Seattle: Sound Resource Management Group.

National Solid Wastes Management Association, 1991. Resource Recovery in North America. Washington, DC: National Solid Wastes Management Association. [contact NSWMA at http://www.envasns.org/nswma]

Solid Waste Association of North America. 1991. *Municipal Solid Waste: An Energy Resource*. Silver Spring, Maryland: Solid Waste Association of North America. [contact SWANA at http://www.swana.org/]

Web Sites

EnerWaste Incineration Systems: http://www.enerwaste.com/

ENVIRONMENTAL JUSTICE

Web Sites

Alternatives for Community and Environment: http://www.pw1.netcom.com/~psloh/ace.html

EcoJustice Network: http://www.igc.apc.org/envjustice/

Indigenous Environmental Network: http://www.alphadc.com/ien/

United States Environmental Protection Agency, Office of Solid Waste and Emergency Response, Environmental Justice: http://www.epa.gov/swerosps/ej/

United States Environmental Protection Agency, Office of Enforcement and Compliance Assurance, Environmental Justice: http://es.epa.gov/oeca/oej/

STYROFOAM, CFCS, AND OZONE DEPLETION

Publications

SIRS, Inc., and the University Corporation for Atmospheric Research. 1994. Ozone: the molecule that protects and destroys. *Science Now Newsletter* 2 (December): 2. [also available at http://www.sirs.com/corporate/newsletters/snow/snow1294/snow1294.htm]

Web Sites

Polystyrene Packaging Council: http://www.polystyrene.org/

WinCup (foam container manufacturer): http://www.wincup.com/

United States Environmental Protection Agency, Great Lakes, Chlorofluorocarbons: http://www.epa.gov/grtlakes/seahome/housewaste/house/chlorofl.htm

Disposal

Background Information

What happens when you throw something away? That product—whether it is a telephone, a pencil, a T-shirt, a cup, or leftover food—becomes part of the municipal waste stream. Municipal solid waste (MSW), more commonly known as trash or garbage, consists of everyday items such as product packaging, grass clippings, furniture, clothing, bottles, food scraps, newspapers, appliances, paint, and batteries. There are several paths that MSW can take: recycling, composting, landfilling, or incineration.

Recycling

Recycling reduces the amount of waste going into landfills, and also relieves the burden on our natural resources. The rate of recycling continues to increase in this country. In 1997, recycling reduced the solid waste stream in the United States by 61 million tons. Recycling is more widespread than ever, thanks to several factors. First, communities across the country are facing shrinking landfill space and must use recycling to reduce the amount of solid waste headed for landfills. Second, industry continues to see higher costs of harvesting virgin material as our natural resource supply dwindles, at the same time that technology improves and lowers the cost of using recycled materials. Third, as the public becomes aware of both limited landfill space and dwindling natural resources, the demand for recycled materials continues to grow, increasing the supply of recycled products.

Topic: recycling

Go to: www.scilinks.org

Code: LCS07

Composting

Gardeners and farmers have long relied on reusing compost made from manure and decaying plants to enrich depleted soil. Recent interest in organic gardening has increased the use of composting instead of adding more chemicals to fertilize the soil. Composting not only reduces chemical use but also prevents organic, decomposable material from taking up landfill space. Yard trimmings and food waste made up nearly 40 percent of the municipal solid waste generated in 1997. Much of those trimmings and waste could have been composted to save valuable landfill space, and would have provided additional benefits for agriculture.

Landfills

In 1997, approximately 55 percent of America's trash ended up in landfills. Paper is the greatest single occupant of landfill space. Although they are easily recycled, newspapers take up 10 to 15 percent of landfill space. You saw that organic material quickly decomposed under the right conditions in a compost pile. In a landfill, organic material can take decades to decompose.

Toxic Leachates

Leachates are formed as the result of interaction with the acid water produced by decomposition within the landfill—paper dyes and chemicals remaining in the paper can dissolve, become mobile, and seep into groundwater. This is why modern landfills are lined with plastic and have fluid-collection wells to monitor any harmful products released. The wells can be pumped and the hazardous/toxic solution(s) removed for treatment, usually in a hazardous waste incinerator.

Landfills are a way to store solid waste, but these facilities can produce different kinds of environmental hazards. Millions of tons of garbage stink; they also attracts pests such as rats and flies. To prevent this, landfills are covered with a layer of soil each night to reduce the odor and deter pests at the landfill. Waterproof materials such as clay line the underside of modern landfills to catch leachate—liquid seepage that may contain toxic chemicals—and prevent it from flowing into the local groundwater. The captured leachate is tested for the presence of toxic chemicals and treated before it is released into the environment.

Another byproduct of landfills is the methane gas produced by decaying organic matter. Methane is an ozone-destroying greenhouse gas; some landfills now capture the gas to prevent its release into the atmosphere and harness the methane for other uses.

Incineration

Besides recycling and composting efforts to divert solid waste, the alternative to landfilling solid waste is incineration. Incinerators process 12 to 17 percent of the trash collected in the United States. This is the most expensive method of solid waste disposal. Incinerators burn the combustible materials in trash and can reduce the mass and volume of solid waste by as much as 90 percent. The residual ash from an incinerator must still be disposed of in a landfill, but the ash occupies far less space in a landfill than raw trash.

Incinerators have a negative image as air polluters. The byproducts of incinerating garbage include NO_x and SO_2, two of the components of acid rain. Modern incinerators monitor the gases that exit their stacks. Gases from the burned trash pass through a scrubber that removes the NO_x and SO_2. Other hazardous byproducts are removed from the gases and from the residual ash. Just as landfills are finding a way to capture and use the gas released from the decomposition of solid waste, incinerators harness the energy released from burning trash.

Energy Gained from Recycling vs. Incineration

Table 6.1 shows the energy requirements for processing and manufacturing some common materials.

Table 6.1: Energy of Production

Material	Typical Product	Energy to Produce 1 Ton (MJs)*
Glass	2 L bottle	14,400
Paper	9 gal. grocery bag	34,400
PET plastic	9 gal. grocery bag	95,600
Copper	Pipe	149,000
Aluminum	12 oz. can	198,200

* Note: To covert to metric tons multiply the number of tons by 0.907185

Reclaiming and recycling are ways to create a new product without using virgin natural resources. But recycling addresses another environmental concern: energy use. Plastics have the same energy content as coal or oil. Energy content is the amount of energy that can be generated from the combustion of materials such as coal, oil, and the components of municipal waste (which are 80 percent combustible). Combustion produces energy in high-temperature incinerators. Water is converted to steam, which in turn drives turbines to produce electricity.

Table 6.2 contrasts the energy savings for recycling and incinerating several materials. Locate copper and PVC plastic—the main components of a telephone that we've studied. Notice that the energy saving is much higher for copper due to its high energy input in the refining process. Metals like copper require large amounts of energy to produce. Heating metal ores (called *roasting*) to high temperatures to separate them from their compounds expends large amounts of energy. Once separated, very high temperatures are used to melt and further purify the metal. Some metals, like aluminum and sodium, are electrolyzed using molten salts. Since acquiring and processing copper requires a lot of money, energy, and time, recycling and reclaiming copper are necessary alternatives to using raw copper ore for each new product.

Table 6.2: Energy Saved in Recycling vs. Incinerating Various Materials

Material	Energy Saved by Recycling (MJ/ton) *	Energy Generated During Incineration	Relative Savings by Recycling vs. Incineration
PAPER			
Newspaper	22,398	8,444	2.7:1
Corrugated paperboard	22,887	7,388	3.1:1
Office paper	35,242	8,233	4.3:1
Other paper	21,213	7,600	2.8:1
PLASTICS			
PET[1]	85,888	21,004	4.1:1
HDPE[2] and PVC	74,316	21,004	3.5:1
Other containers	62,918	16,782	3.7:1
Film/packaging	75,479	14,566	5.2:1
Other rigid plastics	68,878	16,782	4.1:1

Material	Energy Saved by Recycling (MJ/ton) *	Energy Generated During Incineration (MJ/ton) *	Relative Savings by Recycling vs. Incineration
GLASS			
Containers	10,630	3,212	3:1
Other	582	106	5.5:1
METALS			
Aluminum cans	256,830	739	348:1
Other aluminum	281,231	317	888:1
Copper and other non-ferrous metals	116,288	317	367:1
Tin/bi-metal metals	22,097	739	29.9:1
Other ferrous metals	17,857	317	563:1
ORGANICS			
Food waste	4,215	2,744	1.5:1
Yard waste	3,556	3,166	1.1:1
Wood waste	6,422	7,072	0.9:1
RUBBER			
Tires	32,531	14,777	2.2:1
Other	25,672	11,505	2.2:1
TEXTILES			
Cotton	42,101	7,283	5.8:1
Synthetics	58,292	7,283	8.0:1
MIXED			
Diapers	10,962	10,713	1.0:1

[1] polyethylene terephalate
[2] high-density polyethylene
* Note: To covert to metric tons multiply the number of tons by 0.907185

Source: Jeffrey Morris and Diane Canzeroni, **Recycling Versus Incineration: An Energy Conservation Analysis** (Seattle: Sound Resource Management Group, 1992)

A Tale of Two Cups

Procedure/Questions

1. If you had to choose between a polystyrene foam cup and a paper cup of equal size to use once and then throw away, which cup would you choose and why? **Record your answers to all questions in your lab journal.**

Recycling

2. Look carefully at the paper and foam cups. List the materials that make up each cup:

   <u>Paper Cup</u>   <u>Foam Cup</u>

3. Which cup is physically easier to recycle, and why? Ignore what is actually recycled in your community.

Landfills

4. Estimate how many paper and foam cups you use in a typical week. Remember to include cups used in your school cafeteria, fast food restaurants, movies, convenience stores, and at home. Then multiply each estimate by 52 to calculate the number of cups you use in a year. Show your calculations.

   Estimated number of paper cups used in one week: _____ x 52 = _____

   Estimated number of foam cups used in one week: _____ x 52 = _____

   Estimated number of paper cups used in one year: _____ x 52 = _____

   Estimated number of foam cups used in one year: _____ x 52 = _____

5. Use the heel of your shoe to compress each cup as much as possible. Measure the dimensions (length, width, and height in centimeters) and then calculate the volume of each cup. Multiply the volume of each cup by the estimated number of cups used in one year. Show your calculations.

Purpose

In this activity, you will examine the disposal options of two cups. Which cup do you choose?

Materials

- Polystyrene foam cup
- Paper cup
- Ruler

Volume of paper cup: _____ cm³

Volume of foam cup: _____ cm³

Volume of paper cups used in one year: _____ cm³

Volume of foam cups used in one year: _____ cm³

6. What do the final answers of Question 5 represent? Based on those calculations, which cup would you choose if you were considering landfill space?

Incineration

Use Tables 6.1 and 6.2 from your Reading to answer Questions 7–10.

7. Using the data in Tables 6.1 and 6.2, explain why recycling materials into new products requires less energy than acquiring and processing virgin raw materials.

8. What do the second and third columns in Table 6.2 represent, and how are those values measured? What does the last column mean, and how is that value calculated?

9. What does Table 6.2 say about recycling vs. incinerating paper, and recycling vs. incinerating plastic?

10. Combine the data in the two tables to discuss overall energy use and savings for acquiring and disposing of paper and polyethylene terephalate (PET).

Conclusions

11. Your paper cup is made of paperboard, which fits into the "Other paper" category in Table 6.2. Your foam cup is made of polystyrene, which is very similar to PET plastic. If you use a foam cup, how should you dispose of it? If you use a paper cup, how should you dispose of it? Give numbers to support your answer.

12. Having analyzed all the end-of-life options for foam cups and paper cups, choose one cup that you would use and specify the most environmentally friendly way to dispose of it. Explain your reasoning.

13. Although it is possible to recycle paperboard and polystyrene foam, few communities actually do. The Environmental Protection Agency's *Municipal Solid Waste Factbook* gives statistics on the country's solid waste. Go to the *MSW Factbook* Web site, http://www.epa.gov/epaoswer/non-hw/muncpl/factbook/internet/, or use the data saved on your computer or printed out by your teacher. Research recycling, incineration, and landfills in your region of the country.

14. Given the regional statistics from EPA's *Municipal Solid Waste Factbook*, which cup will you choose to use? Explain your reasoning. Your choice may include other factors that are unrelated to the end-of-life stage of a cup's life cycle.

Purpose

After your phone stops working, what happens to it? You will examine the components of the telephone to explore some possible end-of-life uses for your phone.

Materials

- telephones

- list of phone components from Unit Two

- balance

Where Does a Telephone Go When It Dies?

Procedure

1. Discuss as a group what might happen to an old telephone. Answer Question 1 below. **Record all answers in your lab journal.**

2. Examine the phone and your list of phone components. Answer Question 2.

3. As a group, read question 3, and decide who will be responsible for each of the four areas of research. Conduct the research and share your results with your group members.

4. Complete Question 4, as directed by your teacher.

Questions

1. What are some end-of-life options for a used telephone?

2. Give a rough estimate of how long the components (use broad categories) of your phone would last in a landfill using the chart below as a guideline:

   Time needed for the decomposition of some common objects in a landfill:

Banana/orange peel	2-5 weeks
Leather	1 year
Newspaper	up to 50 years
Aluminum can	80-100 years
Plastic bottle	100-200 years
Glass bottle	1,000,000 years

   (Source: *The Garbage Project*, William Rathje, 1990)

3. As a group select one person to:

    •   Research on the World Wide Web the company that produced your phone. Find out what they consider to be the useful life for their phone and what their policy might be in accepting these phones back for recycling.

    •   Contact your school's business office and research what kind of phone system is used in your school. Find out how long they think it will be useful and what is usually done with the system when it is replaced.

    •   Contact a local recycling center and ask them if they accept old phones. Contact a metals salvage dealer to see what you can learn about their recycling practices and what they know about the fate of old telephones.

    •   Contact your local waste management agency/company and ask them what their policy is regarding discarded telephones.

    After you have done your research, write a one- to two-page report to share with your group. Include who you contacted, the date, and what information you obtained. Then, discuss whether you consider your findings to be a good choice for the end-of-life for the telephone.

4. Write a one-page article for your local newspaper that summarizes the results of your group's research and give your recommendations for what should be done with old telephones.

Redesigning a Product

Summary

How can materials be redesigned by incorporating economic and environmental criteria into their life cycle? Students examine the strengths and weaknesses of life cycle assessment for incorporating different values in the design of a product. They use a telephone to examine the practice of sustainable design, then develop their own criteria for evaluating a product. This unit is an assessment of student learning. Student teams present the results of their research that began in Unit One. By analyzing the design of the telephone from each stage of its life cycle, students can synthesize the basic concepts of this book.

Objectives

- To examine the strengths and weaknesses of life cycle assessment for incorporating different values in the design of a product

- To examine the practice of sustainable design

- To redesign a telephone using knowledge gained from the first six *Life Cycle* units

Preparation

This activity is an assessment of what your students have learned about life cycle assessment. As time permits, you can use the first day of the unit to focus students on the major concepts of a life cycle and how design plays a key role. This will serve to refocus their attention on what their reports should include.

Display the *Life Cycle of a Pencil* poster. Place telephones around the classroom for students to observe during this activity. Provide colored pencils for revising the sketch of a telephone's life cycle. Duplicate enough copies of **Student Sheet 7.1, A New Life for an Old Phone**.

The concept of sustainable design is probably new to most students. It involves consideration of the entire life cycle of a product using a set of criteria that have been agreed on by a group. These criteria reflect economic priorities and environmental goals that provide for the needs of the present generation, while also considering the long-term needs and environmental quality for future generations. The goal of sustainable design is to develop products that require lower amounts of total energy in their manufacture and use—throughout their life cycle—and to minimize the deleterious effects of harmful emissions and wastes on the environment.

Teaching Sequence

Day One

Step One: Revisit the *Life Cycle of a Pencil* poster. Quickly go over the life cycle sequence, asking students to call out some of the things that happen at each step in the sequence. Point out that the poster presents a limited view of the life cycle of a product, and students now know enough to improve on it.

Call attention to the telephones you placed around the room. Briefly review what is involved in each step of the cycle of a telephone. Look at the diagrams the students created to represent the life cycle of a product in **Student Sheet 1.1, Introduction to Life Cycles—Matter and Energy Transformations** from Unit One. Ask students to reflect on how their thinking about the life cycle of a product has changed. What have they learned from the activities investigating the various stages of a life cycle?

Step Two: Develop and reinforce the idea that design—the process of selecting the materials and using them to create a useful product that people will buy—is an overriding concept in the life cycle of any product. Challenge the class to consider how they might use what they have learned to redesign the telephone.

Begin this discussion by asking them to suggest what they consider to be the most important factors when creating any new product. Have them consult their lab journals for ideas. Make a list of these on the board. Some criteria include:

1. Use of renewable natural resources
2. Total energy used
3. Total impact on human health
4. Total environmental impact— including toxic emissions to air, water, and land
5. Amount of solid waste generated in product's life
6. Cost to the consumer
7. Aesthetic appeal of product
8. Product function
9. Duration of product's useful life

Time Management

Three to four class periods

Materials

- Completed **Student Sheet 1.2, What's in a Product and Where Does it Go?**
- Completed **Student Sheet 2.2, The Functions and Design Rationale of Telephone Components**
- Colored pencils
- Telephones from Unit Two
- Blank white paper (for creating the telephone's life cycle)

Step Three: Hand out **Student Sheet 7.1** and have students read through the procedure. Have them begin with Procedure Step 1 by drawing their diagram of a telephone's life cycle. They can use the colored pencils to show where energy is added and wastes are generated, or as they like, to create a more dramatic life cycle. Then have them answer Questions 1 and 2 in their lab journals.

Have them review Procedure Steps 2 and 3 as homework for the next day. Stress that they may want to make notes in their lab journals on how to complete the project

Day Two

Step Four: Begin by reviewing Procedure Step 2. Tell them that these are called *design criteria* and incorporate some of the considerations they discussed earlier. Emphasize human impacts on the environment along with some practical considerations such as durability and the ability to be recycled. Have them gather in groups of five to select their first, second, and third choices and write them in **Table 7.1, Ranking Design Priorities**, where the first, second, and third boxes under "Group Rank" reflect their priorities. Stress that it is important to give a reason for each of their choices.

Then as a class, by a show of hands from one member of each group, develop a class ranking, from most to least important. Select the top three and have them place the new ranks in the last column. Have students answer Questions 3 and 4.

Step Five: Discuss the answers to the Questions 1–4 (see below) by emphasizing that each person can benefit from the knowledge of others and that decisions are never based solely on any one factor. The ranking of the group and by the class reflects a compromise.

Have students complete Procedure 3 by completing **Table 7.2, Checklist for Redesigning a Telephone**. As a checklist for how they would change the design of their phone, they can fill in the blank areas, where they see the need to redesign a process or alter the wastes or energy used.

Have students complete Questions 5–7, then lead a discussion of why life cycle assessment can provide mixed results. Develop the idea that it is very important to measure energy, waste, and economic factors carefully—a small error in one of these measurements can produce very different results later in the final analysis of the product. For example, if we were to measure the energy consumption of a telephone only during the hours from midnight to 6 a.m., we would get a very low estimate of total energy consumed. Also, point out that the environmental indicators used are sometimes fuzzy or are not yet supported by real data. Changing costs and sources of energy also affect the estimate of energy values. Environmental issues such as acid rain potential and greenhouse gas generation have not been adopted in every life cycle assessment. The priority one gives to each will greatly affect the results and implications of the life cycle assessment.

Summarize today's work by emphasizing the connection of the design process to the total life cycle. Emphasize that when we consider the redesign of any product, it immediately leads us again to a consideration of the raw materials used and a reconsideration of the manufacturing process. Design is critical to the life cycle and is the overarching concept needed to bring about a truly sustainable economy and a livable environment.

Days Three and Four

Step Six: Hand out **Student Sheet 7.2, Class Presentation Guide and Scoring Rubrics**, which describes the guidelines for written reports and class presentations. Give students two nights to complete their projects. The scoring rubric is included to show students how you will evaluate them. If you wish, the class can grade the oral and visual presentations. You may wish to have student groups fill in the scoring rubrics for each presentation. Before the presentations begin, again review with the class what each rubric means and how you will be relating the assessment of their report to their final grade for this work. The rubrics are included at the end of this unit for ease of duplication.

Answers to Student Sheets and Suggestions for Class Discussion

Student Sheet 7.1

1. *What part of a telephone's life cycle produces the most waste? What part uses the most energy?*

   The manufacture creates the most wastes and the long-term use of the telephone consumes the most energy.

2. *How would you change the design of a telephone to reduce energy and minimize the amount of energy needed in each stage of its life cycle?*

   Answers will vary.

3. *How did your group's ranking compare to the class ranking? Why are there differences? Did you change your ranking after listening to other people's ideas? Why or why not?*

   Answers will vary.

4. *How do we make decisions about important environmental issues as a community or a society? Do you think these decisions should be based solely on scientific evidence or should they include other factors?*

   In discussing Question 4, it is important to emphasize that along with scientific evidence, people must always consider the economic, societal, and personal factors that they value. No decision is based on any one of these, but it should first use the best scientific evidence as the basis for any discussion of the issues and criteria selected for a product's design. Point out that each person, community, and nation has different priorities based on the financial abilities to produce change, the understanding of the problem, and the political desire to affect long-term change. Discuss the various priorities of countries around the world.

5. *Summarize what you have learned about life cycle assessment and how you used this process to redesign your new telephone.*

   Check student work as an assessment of their understanding of the life cycle. Students should consider using new materials, reducing the size of the phone, and going from a phone with cords to one with none. Clearly, future phones will all be cellular in design or use direct transmission from satellites. The energy requirements will be greatly reduced and the need for cable access to homes reduced.

6. *How can some of the assumptions you made about energy usage and waste disposal influence the design of a new phone?*

Check to see if there is a clear connection between energy usage and how the design would be influenced at each stage. Do the same for wastes generated and their disposal.

7. *What do you think are the strengths and weaknesses of life cycle assessment?*

Life cycle assessment (LCA) gives us a valuable tool to begin considerations of the sustainability of the products we create. Even in its rough form, LCA allows designers to rethink materials and the processes used to create these materials and to consider alternatives that minimize energy and wastes. LCA provides a new tool to consider the long-term consequences of single-use products such as disposable diapers and plastic and paper cups. LCA assumptions may be faulty and need great refinement. Today, it is very expensive to examine every aspect of a product's life. Little is actually known about what happens to most products after they are sold to end-users. Society's priorities often change; sometimes land and water pollution may become important and airborne emissions may have a lower priority. LCA may never be done due to costs and the economic need to produce a product at the lower cost, especially in underdeveloped countries. LCA decisions will increasingly exact a greater toll on the environment but, more importantly, on societies that cannot afford the product analyses that technologically advanced countries can implement today. Perhaps the best solution is to export new technologies that will protect future generations from environmental degradation and will conserve important natural resources for all people.

Learning Goals

Unit Seven has been constructed as a summative investigation of *The Life Cycle of Everyday Stuff*'s Learning Goals. Much of students' thinking and learning from other units may be brought to bear as students redesign a telephone. Still, the instructional method used in Unit 7 offers additional routes to address the following Learning Goals.

Enduring understandings

- *Technological design has far-reaching effects.*
- *Materials from human societies affect both the physical and chemical cycles of the Earth.*

Important facts and skills

- *Each component of a telephone has its own design constraints, as does the final telephone.*
- *Each product has a design history; the history influences what the current product does and what it looks like.*
- *Energy is one of the limiting factors of design.*
- *Many people contribute to the design of any product, including the telephone.*

Worth being familiar with

- *There are several ways to approach design problems.*

These Unit Seven Learning Goals contribute to student learning of the following *National Science Education Standards* and *Benchmarks for Science Literacy*.

National Science Education Standards

Science as Inquiry: Content Standard A
     Abilities necessary to do scientific inquiry
     Understandings about scientific inquiry
Science and Technology: Content Standard E
     Abilities of technological design
     Understandings about science and technology
Science in Personal and Social Perspectives: Content Standard F
     Environmental quality: Material from human societies affects both physical
     and chemical cycles of the Earth
     Science and technology in local, national, and global challenges

Benchmarks for Science Literacy

3 The Nature of Technology
     3A Technology and science
     3B Design and systems
8 The Designed World
     8B Materials and manufacturing
     8D Communication
12 Habits of Mind
     12D Communication skills

A New Life for an Old Phone

Procedure

1. On a blank piece of paper, make a sketch of the life cycle of a telephone. Look through your lab journal and recall what you have learned about each stage of its life cycle: raw materials acquisition, manufacturing, packaging and transportation, useful life, and end of life. Use the colored pencils to highlight energy use and waste disposal at each step. Use one color for energy use and another for waste disposal. **Answer Questions 1 and 2 below in your lab journal.**

2. Your group has been selected as the general design company to create an entirely new telephone. As part of your contract with World Wide Telecomm, you are to select from the design guidelines below, the three most important guidelines you will use in redesigning your phone. Discuss these as a group, and write them in the first column of **Table 7.1**, ranked from first to third. After the class discussion, **answer Questions 3 and 4 in your lab journal.**

Purpose

You will apply what you have learned about the life cycle of a product to redesign the telephone.

Materials

- Colored pencils
- Blank paper
- Telephone

Table 7.1: Ranking Design Priorities

Guideline	Reason	Group Rank	Class Rank
	1		
	2		
	3		

3. Use the checklist in **Table 7.2** and the Generalized Design Guidelines to make changes to your life cycle diagram. In each empty box, where appropriate, write in a reason for reducing wastes, minimizing energy, or selecting a different material. Describe on the back of the diagram what your new telephone would look like, or draw it and give the reasons you selected for its new design. Answer Questions 5–7.

4. You should plan to meet after each unit of study to discuss what you have learned about your role, in this part of the telephone's life cycle. In preparation for your final presentation, you should meet several times to share your ideas. You should be able to use your role's point of view to help your team to determine what should be considered in a new design of the telephone. The team design presentation will be a compromise that takes the most important recommendations from each role into consideration.

Table 7.2: Checklist for Redesigning a Telephone

Stage	Materials Choice	Energy Use	Solid Wastes	Waterborne Wastes	Airborne Emissions
Raw Material Acquisition					
Manufacturing, Packaging, and Distribution					
Useful Life					
End-of-Life—Disposal or Reuse					

Generalized Design Guidelines

1. Minimize the use of hazardous, toxic, or other environmentally unfriendly materials.

2. Minimize and recycle residues and waste.

3. Minimize use of energy-intensive process steps or materials.

4. Decrease amount of harmful gaseous, liquid, or solid emissions.

5. Optimize lifetime of product by increasing reliability and durability.

6. Design for easier maintenance and repair.

7. Use recycled materials where possible.

8. Reduce total cost of each phone to the consumer.

Questions

1. What part of a telephone's life cycle produces the most waste? What part uses the most energy?

2. How would you change the design of a telephone to reduce energy and minimize the amount of energy needed in each stage of its life cycle?

3. How did your group's ranking compare to the class ranking? Why are there differences? Did you change your ranking after listening to other people's ideas? Why or why not?

4. How do we make decisions about important environmental issues as a community or a society? Do you think these decisions should be based solely on scientific evidence or should they include other factors?

5. Summarize what you have learned about life cycle assessment and how you used this process to redesign your new telephone.

6. How can some of the assumptions you made about energy usage and waste disposal influence the design of a new phone?

7. What do you think are the strengths and weaknesses of life cycle assessment?

Class Presentation Guide and Scoring Rubrics

Using the information you gathered in **Student Sheet 7.1, A New Life for an Old Phone**, your team will make a presentation to the class on your research and thinking about the redesign of a telephone. You may design your presentation in any way you wish, as long as it meets the following requirements:

- Your group's oral presentation is five to seven minutes long.

- Your group's written report is five to six typed, double-spaced pages, not including a complete bibliography.

- Each group member contributes something to the oral presentation, and the report lists what each person did.

- Your group presents each of the five viewpoints.

- Your group uses a visual aid such as a poster, slides, video, or a PowerPoint® presentation.

In preparation for your final presentation, you should meet with your team at least once to share your ideas. You should be able to use your role's point of view to help your team to determine what should be considered in a new design of a telephone. The team design presentation will be a compromise that takes the most important recommendation from each role into consideration.

The charts that follow show the criteria your teacher will use to grade the presentations.

Written Presentation Rubric

	Good 5 points	Acceptable 3 – 4 points	Needs Improvement 1 – 2 points	Not Done 0 points	Score
Roles	All roles are represented; relative importance of each role in design is evaluated.	All roles are represented.	Some roles are not represented.	No roles are presented.	
Contribution	Proof of each member's unique contribution is given.	Three or four people completed this task.	One or two people completed this task.	Evidence of group contribution is missing.	
Literature Search	Evidence is given that a variety of sources contributed to team conclusions.	Evidence is given that more than one source was used.	One or no sources are referenced in presentation.	No sources are referenced.	
Quality	Team gives a coherent plan for future design, including challenges to implementing the plan.	Team gives a coherent plan for future design.	Team has incomplete plan, missing important details.	No plan is given.	
Length	Presentation is between five and six pages long.	Presentation is more than eight pages or less than five pages long.	Presentation is less than five pages long.	No presentation is given.	
Accuracy	Coverage is thorough and resources are cited.	Some material is missing.	Coverage is incomplete and no references are cited.	Resources section is missing.	

Overall Score

_____

Oral Presentation Rubric

	Good 5 points	Acceptable 3 – 4 points	Needs Improvement 1 – 2 points	Not Done 0 points	Score
Roles	All roles are represented; relative importance of each role in design is evaluated.	All roles are represented.	Some roles are not represented.	No roles are presented.	
Each team member contributes.	Proof of each member's unique contribution is given.	Two or three people completed this task.	One or two people completed this task.	Evidence of group contribution is missing.	
Presentation meets time requirements.	Presentation is between five and seven minutes long.	Presentation is over eight minutes or less than five minutes long.	Presentation is grossly over or under desired time.	No presentation is given.	
Presentation engages the audience.	Presentation excites/fully engages the audience.	Presentation engages the audience most of the time.	Some engagement, but presentation is uneven.	Presentation is boring.	
Quality of conclusions	Team gives a coherent plan for redesign, including challenges to implementing plan.	Team gives a coherent plan for redesign.	Team has incomplete plan, missing important details.	No plan is given.	

Overall Score

_____

Visual Presentation Rubric

	Good 5 points	Acceptable 3 – 4 points	Needs Improvement 1 – 2 points	Not Done 0 points	Score
Role	All roles are represented; each can be clearly under-stood and evaluated by the audience.	All roles are represented.	Some roles are not represented.	No roles are presented.	
The presenta-tion media is easily compre-hended by the audience.	Easy to see major components presented and comprehend their placement.	Presentation is somewhat easy to see and comprehend.	Difficult to see components by order/arrangement or some are missing.	Disorganized or major parts are missing.	
Presentation shows creativity.	Approach is highly creative.	Visuals are somewhat creative.	Creativity is below average.	No creativity is shown.	

Overall Score

_____

NSTA would be interested in sharing your class' research in the revision of this book.
Please mail your comments to: NSTA Press, 1840 Wilson Boulevard, Arlington, VA 22201-3000.